DISCOVERING
BIRDS

DISCOVERING
BIRDS

— *Rob Hume* —

*The RSPB guide to finding
and enjoying birds in any patch of countryside
anywhere in Europe*

Thanks

To Andrew and Mel and my wife, Marcella, for constant encouragement.

First published in Great Britain in 1992 by

The Royal Society for the Protection of Birds
The Lodge, Sandy, Bedfordshire, SG19 2DL

Copyright © Rob Hume 1992
© Duncan Petersen Publishing Ltd 1992

© Artwork Ian Wallace, Darren Rees, John Busby, Peter Partington 1992

Concept by Rob Hume

Bird artwork by Ian Wallace, Darren Rees, John Busby, Peter Partington

Edited, designed and produced by
Duncan Petersen Publishing Ltd,
54, Milson Road,
London, W14 0LB

Originated in Hong Kong by Regent Publishing Services Ltd

Printed in Italy by Arnoldo Mondadori, Verona

A CIP catalogue record of this book is available at the British Library

Editorial director	Andrew Duncan
Assistant editor	Joshua Dubin
Art director	Mel Petersen
Designers	Chris Foley, Beverley Stewart

ISBN 0 903138 53 0

Picture Credits

AA Picture Library: 47, 137, 207, 231 – Barrie Smith: 179; Hansgeorg Arndt: 210 (bottom); **Aquila** – Abraham Cardwell: 33 – E. A. James: 171 – Alan Richards: 55, 111 – Jim Sowerby: 59 – J. Mathieson: 79; L. Campbell: 13, 31, 183, 205, 211, 213, 217; D. Garner: 15, 80 (top), 103, 105, 161, 175; J. V. & G. R. Harrison: 139, 151, 177; R. A. Hume: 29, 71, 201, 225, 233; E. A. Janes: 19, 23, 69, 135, 143, 147, 163; Gordon Langsbury: 57, 116 (top), 152 (middle); Joy Langsbury: 93, 141; Richard T. Mills: 145; A. T. Moffett: 1, 116 (bottom), 152 (top), (bottom), 153, 210 (top); **NHPA** – L. Campbell: 41 – J. S. Gifford: 43 – Brian Hawkes: 49 – David Woodfall: 2, 73, 119, 127, 165, 169, 195, 199 – Stephen Dalton: 109 – E. Murtomäki: 155 – N. A. Callow: 223 – Pierre Petit: 227; **Oxford Scientific Films** – Tony Bomford: 83; R. K. Packwood: 107; Jonathan Plant: 37, 67, 77, 125, 209, 229; Richard Revels: 14, 21, 22, 25, 39, 61, 123, 187, 191, 193, 197; **RSPB:** 167, 189; M. Edwards: 219 – C. H. Gomersall: 3, 7, 11, 14 (bottom), 16, 17 (top & bottom), 18, 27, 45, 51, 65, 75, 80 (bottom), 85, 95, 97, 99, 115, 117, 121, 129, 149, 157, 180, 181, 203, 215, 234 – Michael W. Richards: 63, 101, 113, 173 – A. C. Clay: 131; Colin Varndell: 89, 91, 133, 159, 185

CONTENTS

Please note
The birds in this book are not drawn to scale with each other

Discovering birds

This book is unique in the way it makes the vital connection between birds and the kinds of places where you might expect to see them. Equally important, it gives a useful clue to the sort of place where you are *unlikely* to find many species.

Discovering birds is half the fun of watching them. It takes you into all sorts of wonderful places, from the secluded charm of a bluebell wood in spring to the crumbling splendour of northern coastal cliffs.

Birds are inseparable from place. How can a puffin be at its best if it is not on a ledge of red sandstone, surrounded by tufts of pink thrift? Could a ruin ever be so picturesque without the chatter of jackdaws? Or a cathedral so atmospheric without the comfortable cawing of rooks from the limes above the cloisters?

Identifying birds, and understanding them, is both fascinating and satisfying. But finding them is even more fundamental. *Discovering Birds* is a book devoted to just that.

Lesser black-backed gulls sharply defined in their setting.

6

Using this book

Each two-page spread in the main section of this book illustrates a particular type of habitat found in Europe, northwards to the Arctic Circle, south to Spain, east to Germany and west to the west coast of Ireland.

Most of the habitats illustrated are common and widespread. Some, however, are widespread only at certain latitudes. Others are specific, or restricted, found in but a few places, perhaps even just one locality in Europe. The introductory paragraph (found usually at the top left hand corner of each spread) makes it clear to which category the habitat belongs.

Assume, unless otherwise specifically stated, that the photographs are common and widespread examples of the habitat wherever you happen to be in Europe.

Sequence

The habitats discussed and illustrated in this book are arranged in a sequence that begins on the coast and climbs uphill. In addition, this sequence generally moves from the west and north towards the south and east: from the cold and damp to the hot and sunny.

Europe's natural habitats are not, however, quite so simply arranged in reality. Average temperatures decline towards the north, so that birds of more southerly mountain tops can be found at lower altitudes. This is apparent even over quite small distances. The ptarmigan, found at 3,000 feet (925 m) or more on the Cairngorm plateaux in the eastern highlands of Scotland, can be watched at 1,000 feet (300 m) or less above sea level close to Cape Wrath, on the exposed north-western corner of the Scottish mainland. Rare breeders in Scotland, such as snow bunting and shorelark, are found very much lower down in Scandinavia.

At the same time, towards the interior of mainland Europe, away from the coast, the climate becomes more extreme, with hotter summers but colder winters. The western coastal zone, influenced by the warm sea, has moister, cooler summers than the interior, but is less harsh in winter. The mild estuaries of Britain are less affected by ice than the Baltic (which is less salty) or indeed the Netherlands' landlocked Ijselmeer, which is relatively shallow.

We have tried to select photographs which not only illustrate the habitat faithfully, but which are excellent in their own right – which do justice to the fascination and beauty of landscape. The bird images in the margins are the work of talented wildlife illustrators.

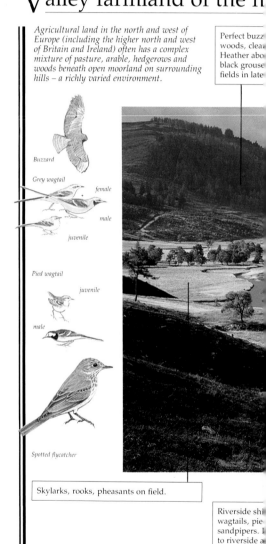

Valley farmland of the n

Agricultural land in the north and west of Europe (including the higher north and west of Britain and Ireland) often has a complex mixture of pasture, arable, hedgerows and woods beneath open moorland on surrounding hills – a richly varied environment.

Perfect buzz
woods, clea
Heather abo
black grouse
fields in late

Buzzard

Grey wagtail

female

male

juvenile

Pied wagtail

juvenile

male

Spotted flycatcher

Skylarks, rooks, pheasants on field.

Riverside sh
wagtails, pie
sandpipers. I
to riverside a

182

Changing seasons

When using this book, bear in mind a few commonsense factors, and in particular the changing seasons.

A wood in spring will resound with the songs of willow warblers, blackcaps, garden warblers,

with mixed
nd, rough slopes.
lopes may have
ture on to open

Valley wood full of small birds such as
spotted flycatchers, chaffinches, willow
warblers, treecreepers, long-tailed, coal,
blue and great tits, thrushes, blackbirds.

Cleared slopes in forest useful for seeing
sparrowhawks, buzzards, crossbills flying
over open space. Scattered trees in rough
grazing chosen as song posts by tree pipits.

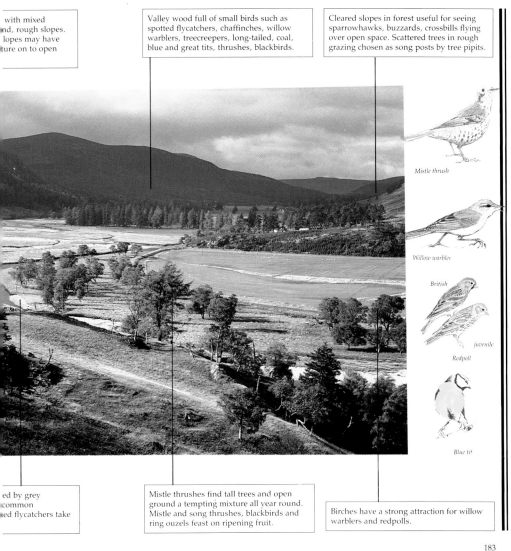

Mistle thrush

Willow warbler

British

juvenile

Redpoll

Blue tit

ed by grey
common
ed flycatchers take

Mistle thrushes find tall trees and open
ground a tempting mixture all year round.
Mistle and song thrushes, blackbirds and
ring ouzels feast on ripening fruit.

Birches have a strong attraction for willow
warblers and redpolls.

183

cuckoos and nightingales, but in winter all will be
gone, possibly to be replaced by bramblings, siskins, fieldfares and redwings.

The captions tell you the bird species you could
expect to see in that habitat. Where the photograph was taken, with a few interesting excep-
tions, is not important: the photographs are
generalized examples of the habitat type, and the
birds mentioned in the captions are found there
and typical of it. If it is significant that a photograph was taken in a specific place the heading and
the introductory paragraph will make this clear.

The birdlife of western Europe

By any standards, birdlife in the area of northern and western Europe covered by this book is remarkable and varied. It includes some of the most densely populated parts of the world, yet its teeming cities, congested roads, vast industrial developments and polluted seas live often cheek by jowl with wonderful habitats for birds.

Autumn migration routes

Britain, Ireland and the countries bordering the North Sea are privileged to lie on the great east Atlantic flyway, the route along which millions of birds migrate south each autumn and return northwards every spring. Millions of waders and wildfowl breeding in a swathe around the Arctic rely on the wetlands and especially the estuaries bordering the North Sea for rest and food on their journeys north and south. Indeed, waders and wildfowl from as far afield as northern Asia funnel westwards and down the west European coast while others from Greenland and Iceland head east before joining this same southward flow.

The Mediterranean also creates, for bird-watchers, a natural trap for birds. It is an obstacle to the millions of migrants that must cross it to reach their African wintering grounds. The smaller species pause on the northern slopes to rest before crossing; the bigger birds, such as storks, can be seen wheeling upwards on currents of warm air to give them height in order to make possible the sea crossing. Dramatic concentrations of soaring storks, vultures, kites, buzzards and eagles appear annually at narrow crossing points such as Gibraltar.

The coasts of Europe have some of the finest congregations of breeding seabirds anywhere in

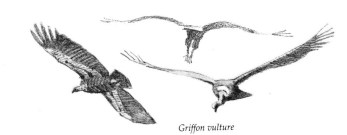

Griffon vulture

Golden eagle

Hen harrier

Alpine accentor

Gannet

Seabird cliffs afford superb opportunities for birdwatching.

the world. The northern and western cliffs of Britain and Ireland offer arguably some of the most important concentrations of birds and many of the most memorable bird experiences of Europe: the thriving seabird cities where thousands of gannets, auks and gulls collect on dramatic sea cliffs. And then there are the nocturnal visits to cliffs and islands by hundreds of thousands of shearwaters and petrels.

Inland, the uplands of Britain and northern Europe have their own fascinating birds, from grouse and golden plovers to hen harriers and golden eagles. The high mountain regions are not only beautiful but good for birds, too, from the bleak, exposed peaks of the Scottish highlands, with their eagles and ptarmigan, to the Alps, where one can hope to see snowfinches, wallcreepers and Alpine choughs, and to the Pyrenees, where high altitude birds such as Alpine accentors are joined by griffon vultures and lammergeiers on their long-range foraging flights.

These high peaks create islands of habitat that resemble the tundra of the far north. In northern Scandinavia true tundra and boreal forest can be found, where select waders, wildfowl, divers and owls breed in remote seclusion. Forests farther south are rich in birds of their own, while many of the woodland species have adapted well to similar, sometimes even better, habitats in towns and villages.

From the cool, damp pastures of the far north, with their breeding shore birds and very restricted numbers of small songbirds, to the hot, dry steppes and Mediterranean slopes in the south, western Europe is varied and exhilarating in its wealth of birds. Many habitats, in particular fragile wetlands and natural forests, are under severe threat from man – indeed, many have long since disappeared. What remains deserves our best efforts to ensure that future generations may, like us, have the happy experience of discovering birds in their natural setting.

11

Understanding habitats

A new-found enthusiasm to get out and see wild birds is all very well. But how do you go about it? Everyday birds present no difficulty; but many species are a challenge – and meeting the challenge is part of the fun.

Whinchat

There are many ways to find birds. One is to exploit a knowledge of their habitat requirements. This book is ideal for that.

The photographic spreads forming the main part of this book will help you better than anything else to read the landscape, and to understand the kinds of habitats in which particular birds need to live. Most do need specific habitats and do not choose to live where they do, in any conscious way. They have evolved over enormous lengths of time to fit specific niches in the environment. If their habitat is threatened, so are they.

This is the basis of modern wildlife conservation. There is no point passing a law to protect a bird if its habitat is not also protected. Getting decision-makers to understand this is crucial, because birds simply cannot survive without their particular food, nest sites, roosting sites and even details such as suitable perches. Knowing this, we can learn to look at the countryside in a new way, trying to relate the features we can see to the needs of birds.

A wide expanse of uniform grass, swaying in

the breeze, may look just right for a 'grassland' species such as the whinchat; but in reality it is not. Whinchats need grassland, true, but they also need a scattering of taller observation posts – young trees, long stems of plants like docks or umbellifers, or fence posts perhaps. They find food by perching in exposed spots and looking for insects. In a sea of tall grass, whinchats are denied perches to give them a suitable view. They are not made to hover overhead, like kestrels, nor to walk through the grass like larks. They cannot, therefore, live in uniform long grass and there is no point either protecting such a habitat for the whinchat, or looking there in the expectation of seeing one.

A pied flycatcher needs a special kind of wood. An oak wood is not, in itself, enough. Oak trees in parks, or dense oaks on a lowland plain, or lovely, giant, rambling old oaks mixed with holly and elder and hornbeam on heavy clay soils, are of little use to a pied flycatcher. It needs tall, upstanding oaks, often growing on poor soils, where heavy grazing by deer, rabbits and sheep and deep shade beneath the high

A variety of features increases the attraction of a landscape for a range of species.

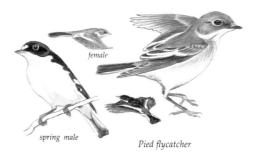

female

spring male   *Pied flycatcher*

canopy keep the forest undergrowth at bay.

Like wood warblers, pied flycatchers need woods with a closed canopy and almost bare ground below, with plenty of open space for their flycatching activities. Look for either of them in the wrong kind of wood, and they will not be there.

13

Understanding habitats/2

Left, a snipe's song post.

Similarly, there will be no nesting guillemots on a coast with soft, sloping earth cliffs, and no grey wagtails nesting beside broad, sluggish lowland rivers. Avocets need soft mud with a gleam of surface water through which to slice their upcurved bills; snipe have to have soft mud for deep probing with their sensitive, straight beaks. Neither will be on shoreline rocks or dry, sun-baked clay. Birds all have their own needs and, by learning them, you will gain insights into where to find them – and where not to bother to look.

Below, an avocet poised characteristically as it feeds.

Certain birds are, it is true, very adaptable – the house sparrow and starling for example. Others are at the opposite extreme. Rarely is a treecreeper seen away from the bark of a tree: few birds are so strictly confined to the same kind of place, all year round. Every treecreeper, everywhere, spends nearly all its life living up to its name, literally creeping about trees, pressed close to the bark. They don't even flit about among the leaves or dash out for a fly.

Nor are dippers ever away from water, although some leave their upland streams in winter and move to broader, deeper waters, occasionally the edges of large lakes and reservoirs, which are less likely to freeze.

Sedge warblers are always in thick, upright vegetation in more or less damp situations and reed warblers are even more strictly tied to waterside plants, in particular reed, although they feed in nearby willows. However, in autumn especially, both may turn up in odd places on migration. Strange things can, and do, happen. But knowing the relationship between a bird and its bush is fundamental to bird-watching.

Sedge warbler

Reed warbler

Dipper

15

Fieldcraft

Even if you know the precise habitat in which to look for a species, catching a glimpse of the bird is not as a rule straightforward. Out of doors, birds are rarely as they appear in books.

Small birds in the tops of tall trees don't show all their colours and detailed patterns. They may be little more than dark dots against a bright sky. Some budding birdwatchers never recover from this frustrating discovery. Waders on the edge of a pool are rarely obliging enough to stay put while you check the colour of their legs and bills, and the extent of their wing bars. They tend, instead, to fly off into the distance as soon as you appear.

Optical equipment

Binoculars are essential, except for some bird-watching in gardens and parks. Get the best you

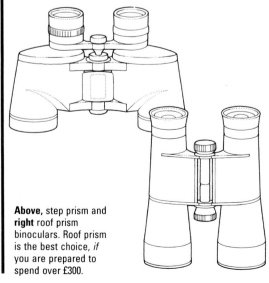

Above, step prism and **right** roof prism binoculars. Roof prism is the best choice, *if* you are prepared to spend over £300.

can afford, with a magnification somewhere between seven and ten – don't be tempted by anything more powerful. Go for 7×50, 8×40, 10×40 or 10×50. The second figure is the diameter of the larger lenses in millimetres. Wider lenses give more light, but make heavier binoculars. Higher magnifications need extra light to give a bright image, have a reduced field of view and don't usually focus particularly close – something to be considered when watching birds in a wood, for example. Choosing the best binoculars for you will always be a compromise.

Take the trouble to get the individual eyepiece adjustment exactly right for you, and practise using them so that focussing becomes second nature. Out of focus or poorly adjusted binoculars give a blurred image in one or both eyes. A surprising number of people persist in using them like that, not realizing what they are missing. Quality binoculars, properly focussed, are a joy to use.

A telescope (best used on a tripod) gives much higher magnification than binoculars, at the expense of a narrower field of view. It is also a much more cumbersome piece of equipment. A telescope is likely to be very useful where birds are far away – on estuaries, reservoirs and so on – but hopeless in the close confines of a wood, when it is best left at home.

Clothing

In general, wear whatever is comfortable. It is far more important to be dry and warm, or cool and free to move, depending on the weather, than to be clad in an outfit that conforms to a birdwatching image. Thick wax jackets, woolly hats and heavy boots are not needed for a walk around the park in summer.

Keep quiet, even behind a screen.

A hide placed to maximum advantage.

White, or bright colours can alert birds to your presence; although being quiet and keeping still are more important than wearing dull colours. For everyday birdwatching, comfort is essential, and plenty of pockets for notebooks, guide books, maps and sandwiches are useful.

Keeping quiet

It is important to be quiet when birdwatching. Birds have excellent hearing and if they hear you approach may move away long before you have seen them. Even in hides at nature reserves, keeping quiet is essential if you are to have close views (and, in any case, is only fair to other birdwatchers). Remember that loudly-hissed whispers carry far, too – best to talk in low, subdued tones.

Keeping still

Birds are ultra-aware of movement. You can often get closer to a bird if you go straight up to it than if you move to one side: there is less apparent movement. But there is no substitute for simply keeping still, especially when getting close. Oddly enough, you can sometimes cruise slowly and quietly past a bird in a car or on a bicycle, and then find that the bird flies off if you stop. It is sudden change that seems to disturb most birds.

Even at long range, some birds react to the sudden appearance of a human. Wildfowl are especially likely to fly off if you suddenly appear at the top of a bank beside a lake or a wet meadow. Keep down, keep out of sight, and keep absolutely still.

In a hide, don't put your arms out and wave them about if you are trying to point out a bird to others. Use a clock system to describe the direction in which to look: 'Four o'clock from the top of the big pine'.

Fieldcraft/2

Use the light

Sunshine can be a help or a hindrance. Looking into the light means birds tend to look dark, silhouetted against the glare. They may look black, but they aren't – they just don't show the colours painted in your book. At the same time, they see you perfectly lit. Better, if you can, to get the sun behind you.

If you are visiting a lake or reservoir, or a large reserve, you can often arrange to be on the right side in the morning and switch round in the afternoon to get the best of the light at all times.

Conversely, you can also use a bright expanse of sky to pick out a bird silhouetted in a hedge or tree. Having pinpointed its location, you can move round to get a better-lit view.

Listen for calls

Bird sounds are of immense importance to birdwatchers. Not only can they identify a bird even before it is seen, but they alert you to the presence of many birds that would otherwise go undetected. The majority of birds in woods or in bushy areas are heard before they are seen and, if they did not call, might be overlooked completely.

Even if you don't know what the calls are, at least follow them up. It is by far the best way to learn them. If you search for a bird making a strange noise in a tree for 15 minutes and it turns out to be a great tit (it usually does), at least you will know next time.

Hobby

Sand Martin

Calls are of great value in other ways. The sudden, sharp 'tik tik' of a starling alerts other starlings – and, therefore, you too – to an approaching sparrowhawk. The loud, excited chattering of swallows and martins announces the appearance of a hobby. Thin, high squeaks from blue or great tits warn their fellows that some predator is about. Often, a roosting owl is discovered by small birds which then kick up a racket around it – known as 'mobbing'. The knowing birdwatcher can find the elusive object of attention.

Watch for movement
Skilled birdwatchers are often told that they must have excellent eyesight or that their binoculars must be of superb quality. The truth, most often, is simply that they are aware of birds, and conscious of movement. In a tree with thousands of leaves blowing in a breeze, a bird hopping the 'wrong' way stands out. Sometimes birds can even be spotted by their shadows or reflections.

It is usually movement of some kind that catches the eye, often the extreme corner of the eye, and it is the experienced birdwatcher's ability to notice it and follow it up, time after

Be prepared for sunlight to affect radically what you see of birds. **Above left** and **above** are contrasting extremes.

time, that gives them the edge. Nothing more than a flicking tail or a hop from twig to twig can lead to something good.

Sparrowhawk

Starling

19

Fieldcraft/3

Stalking

How close you can get depends on the habitat. Clearly, with a reed bed, there is nothing for it but to settle down at the edge and wait. You may find a gap in the reeds, perhaps a ditch or small muddy clearing, and hope the birds come out of the depths; going in after them is hopeless, and damaging.

In bushes and thick scrub, you may well have to adopt the same low-key tactics. But you can quietly, slowly, move around to get the best angle of view. Sometimes, if a bird enters a bush, you can nip round to the other side to wait for it to reappear there. Don't crash in after it: it will go to ground, or slip out without you catching a glimpse. Besides, you may risk damaging its nest. *Patience is the key.*

In woods, go early in the season (when the leaves are still few and far between) and early in the day. In late summer, the dense, dull greenery makes birdwatching hard and the birds have stopped singing. In autumn and winter birds collect in flocks and roam through the woods together, so you see nothing for long spells, then more than you can cope with all at once. Listen and look for the flock and you will find all kinds of interest on a woodland fringe.

You can predict the time and place of waders' arrival at a high-tide roost, and settle down in advance. Sit out of sight, below the skyline, and let the rising tide bring the birds to you. Remember, you have a responsibility not to disturb them at the time they most need their rest. This may mean that you cannot get up to walk away until the tide begins to fall again.

The importance of 'edge'

Solid reeds, dense woods, the middle of a lake or the centre of a mudflat can all harbour birds, but the edges of habitats, or where two or more habitats meet, tend to be the best. There is more variety there and a better chance that your bird will come into the open.

Many woodland birds are really woodland-edge species. These are the ones that have often made a successful transition to suburban garden life. Spotted flycatchers like to sit in a tree but need an open space to fly into to snatch up an insect, perhaps one that gleams in the sun against a dark background. Tree pipits perch in trees and sing from them, but nest and feed on the ground in nearby open space.

You can also exploit the change from one habitat to another. If you approach the edge of a

Kingfisher

Spotted flycatcher

wood, always look carefully, both ways, to see what might scuttle off into the trees as you appear. Do the same if you come to a ditch, stream or track that crosses your route – this is often the best way to pick up a water rail, or a kingfisher, or a grey partridge. Make a habit of 'looking round corners' – along hedges and even roadside verges. Any break in an otherwise uniform landscape is a likely spot for discovering birds.

The value of water

Much birdwatching is linked to watersides of one kind of another. Waders and ducks are obvious waterside birds; so too are wagtails, pipits, buntings, swallows, even warblers and finches, at certain times of the year.

Birds in a wood can be tediously difficult to find, or to see well. Find a drinking pool, instead: sit quietly and wait for what turns up. You may be surprised: it is a special experience to share the company of an elusive bird, as it drinks and bathes.

If there is no suitable pool in your local wood, or even in your garden, you can make one. In hot weather, even a thin trickle of water from a pipe attracts a variety of birds to drink.

Feeding birds

As well as water, birds need food and can be attracted to regular feeding places such as bird tables. Experiment, if you have access to a secluded wood, with feeding stations there, too. You may be able to attract birds to a sunny clearing beside a pine forest, or to a clear space in front of a permanent hide.

Remember, though, that such places will generally have an abundance of natural food and birds may not necessarily take much notice of your offerings. If, on the other hand, they do, you must take account of the degree to which they become dependent on your free handouts. In general, random scattering of food in a wood is unlikely to be of much value.

Below: this meeting of habitats offers rich birdwatching.

Coastlands

Seabirds come to safe sites ashore to breed. Shags, **left**, spectacular gatherings of gannets, **right,** and huge colonies of noisy kittiwakes, **below,** congregate in splendid seabird cities.

A north-western island oasis

North-west European coasts and offshore islands have surprisingly serene, sheltered places with lily-covered lakes and beds of reeds and sedges, providing oases for many birds.

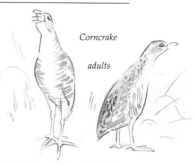

Corncrake

adults

Farmed land is excellent for twites, stonechats, wheatears, reed and corn buntings, tree sparrows. Old hay meadows and iris beds have declining numbers of corncrakes.

Even low Hebridean hills have golden eagles, roaming widely when hunting.

Twite

male

Oystercatcher

Sedge warbler

Sedge warblers prefer deep, wet, and tangled beds of sedges, rushes and herbaceous plants.

juvenile

adult

Common tern

Whooper swans frequent in winter, very rarely staying on in summer. Greylag geese are regular nesters but highly localized nevertheless.

Common terns nest on rocky islets; also oystercatchers, mallards, common scoters.

Shallow lochs with lilies and rushes hold odd pairs of coots, mute swans. Red-necked phalaropes (very rare) nest in the marsh, feeding from the water or along the water's edge.

Greylag goose

Mute swan

Bleak north-western island

North-western coastal moors are cold, windswept and wet and have an Alpine (or northern) quality. Although there are few true tundra birds, the mixture of species is special.

Wonderful breeding wader assemblies include golden plovers, dunlins in wetter parts, whimbrels, curlews, oystercatchers, snipes and lapwings. Red-necked phalaropes are to be seen on certain bogs; they feed on bleak lochs.

Whimbrel

summer

winter

Red-necked phalarope

Red-throated diver

summer

Red-throated divers nest beside tiny moorland pools and fly noisily to and from the sea where they feed. Common and lesser black-backed gulls may be found nesting beside wet flows.

Arctic terns nest on the moorland slopes as well as the tideline rocks.

Arctic tern

Hen harrier

Heathery slopes above damp, rushy valleys used by merlins (hard to see) and hen harriers (often more obvious). Kestrels nest in heather, in the absence of trees.

On the open moor, few small birds apart from meadow pipits. Twites prefer edge of cultivation or deep heather within reach of meadows. Wrens and rock pipits live near the shore.

Snowy owl (very rare) on bleak, rocky moors, often a white dot on a distant stony ridge. Great and Arctic skuas nest on long, rolling, peaty slopes and ridges.

Wren

Snowy owl
male

Great skua

A seabird island

Several islands along the west coasts of France, England and Wales have red sandstone cliffs above clear blue bays, topped by natural rock gardens of coastal flowers: idyllic for seabirds.

Storm petrel

Guillemots and razorbills lay eggs on rocky ledges, kittiwakes in nests of seaweed on sheer cliffs. Storm petrels use small cavities among boulders and dry stone walls.

Guillemot

Razorbill

Kittiwake

Puffins collect in sheltered bays during spring and on most afternoons through the summer. Grass-covered screes and boulder screes are typical puffin nesting areas.

Puffin

Manx shearwater

Lesser black-backed gull

Great black-backed gulls perch on prominent look-outs and chase incoming puffins. On moonlit nights, gulls also attack shearwaters that risk a visit.

Little owls live among the rocks and take storm petrels at night. The short-eared owl hunts by day, seeking voles in the rough growth of thrift, bluebells and campion.

Chough

Holes in hummocky turf are occupied by Manx shearwaters: they stay hidden inside by day, while their mates return from the sea late at night. Lesser black-backed gulls nest on the island slopes.

On cliffs with short heath or close-cropped pasture nearby, there will be choughs. The cliffs echo with their ringing, joyful calls. In autumn they gather in flocks.

Coastal pasture, far north-west

In the mild but windswept north-west, the wild geese arrive each autumn. Pastures enriched especially to attract them have the largest flocks while the green sward lasts.

Slavonian grebe

Lapwing, winter

In winter, the sea lochs hold eiders, mergansers, scaup, occasional long-tailed ducks, great northern and red-throated divers, Slavonian grebes and, with luck, the occasional razorbill.

Scaup, winter male

Low tide brings lapwings, redshanks, curlews, oystercatchers, dunlins, godwits to the beach. At high tide they roost on the fields or highest parts of the saltmarsh.

Smooth green fields with rich grass are a magnet for barnacle and Greenland white-fronted geese. Greenland white-fronts will often favour rushy corners beside stone walls.

White-fronted goose

immature

adult

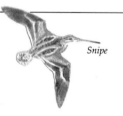

Snipe

The pastures come alive to the drumming of snipes and the songs of curlews, lapwings and skylarks in spring. Black grouse visit the rushy fields to lek.

Skylark

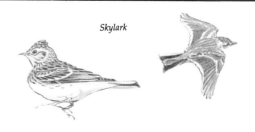

Barnacle goose, adult

Hen harriers hunt along field-edges and ditches, walls and gullies; merlins, kestrels, harriers, buzzards, golden eagles all hunt open ground.

Ragged north-western coast

Western Scotland and parts of the Scandinavian coast are exposed, cold and wet, but often serenely calm and sunny. The landscape is dominated by rock, poor, thin soils and fingers of blue sea edged by beaches of stones and fine sand.

The old raised beach is partly cultivated, partly pasture invaded by bracken; full of pied wagtails, starlings and jackdaws around the sheep, whinchats in the bracken.

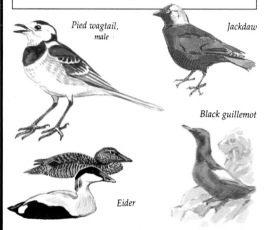

Pied wagtail, male

Jackdaw

Black guillemot

Eider

On the sea, black-throated divers feed in small groups, red-throated in ones and twos. Black guillemots are frequent. Eiders are often to be seen around the seaweed-covered rocks.

A stony storm beach affords occasional feeding for rock pipits, dunlins, turnstones, oystercatchers, curlews. A stretch of sandy beach adds sanderlings, now and then bar-tailed godwits, knots.

Oystercatchers and ringed plovers breed along the upper beach; common gulls nest in the rocks. Common and Arctic terns may choose the beach or offshore islets.

Rock pipit

Oystercatcher

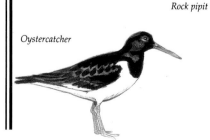

Common gull summer

Corncrake

Wheatear

Golden eagle

Hillsides of cropped grass and loose stones have wheatears, sometimes ring ouzels, meadow pipits, crows. Corncrakes (very rare) might be in the richer vegetation down below.

Ravens nest on hills inland and roam widely everywhere. Higher hills have ptarmigan on exposed rocky plateaux; golden eagles love this mixed country, but food is sparse.

Flat, exposed north-western coast

This hard environment is none the less frequently made habitable by sheltered bays and inlets, and softened by the small villages and patches of farmland nearby.

Look for eiders and red-breasted mergansers in the bays. In winter, scaup and goldeneyes are likely and the odd great northern or red-throated diver may stay for weeks before flying on.

Rock pipit

Wren

Glaucous gull

summer

Great black-backed gull

Gulls are to be seen all year round, but in winter the small harbours are worth checking for visiting glaucous and Iceland gulls amongst the herring and great black-backed gulls.

Such exposed landscape, devoid of trees, holds few small birds – except perhaps meadow and rock pipits, skylarks, wrens in low undergrowth and visiting starlings. Rock doves are common.

Redshank

Rock dove

Crows forage the shorelines as much as the fields. Along seaweed-covered rocks there are grey herons, redshanks, oystercatchers and curlews. Now and then a song thrush feeds nearby.

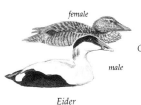

female

male

Eider

Great northern diver, summer

In spring, ring ouzels and wheatears are likely; on the heathery moors inland, golden plovers and curlews are frequently heard songsters.

Grey heron

White-tailed eagle

Black guillemot

Black guillemots enjoy the sheltered, rocky shores of indented northern coasts. Cormorants often fish at the head of the bay, or in large harbours.

White-tailed eagles are rare and localized, breeding along rocky coasts, sometimes visiting these bays in search of fish.

North-western shingle beach

Western and northern shingle beaches often enclose lagoons of brackish water surrounded by rough grazing. Sea and waterside birds abound in such places.

Sandwich tern

autumn

spring

Close-cropped fields by the coast, with rabbit burrows or tumble-down stone walls, often have a pair of wheatears.

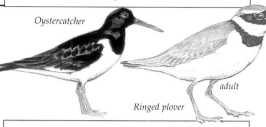

Oystercatcher

Ringed plover

adult

Lagoons behind the shingle beach are sheltered enough for little, Sandwich and common terns to drink and bathe in during the summer.

Ringed plovers hide their eggs among the shingle. Oystercatchers nest on open shingle, or where stones merge with grass.

Common tern, juvenile

Look in the bay for eiders, mergansers and fishing terns. From the headland, spare an hour or so to watch for fishing gannets, passing fulmars, terns, kittiwakes and Manx shearwaters.

Gannet

Stonechat

female

male

Red-breasted merganser

A mixture of grass, exposed sand, bracken and gorse can attract a pair of stonechats.

Manx shearwater

Secluded north-western sea loch

Rocky western shores of Scandinavia and Scotland can have deeply indented bays and sheltered coves where the habitats of shoreline, sea and land birds become closely interlocked.

Redpolls chatter and trill in their looping song flights over coastal woods and crossbills visit the seeding pines.

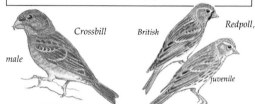

Crossbill *British* *Redpoll,*

male *juvenile*

Rock pipit

Oystercatcher *Common sandpiper*

ARCTIC TERN

Arctic adult

Arctic

Arctic and common terns are very alike. On Arctic look for all-red bill, 'see-through' wing tips with fine dark trailing edge from beneath, all-pale wing tips on top; common has scarlet bill tipped black, see-through patch only behind bend of wing and dark streaks on top of wing tip.

Breeding and migrant common sandpipers and wandering curlews, redshanks, greenshanks and turnstones will feed along the shore.

Oystercatchers pipe noisily along rocky and grassy shores, making the hills echo to their loud calls on calm evenings. They nest on stony places near the tideline.

At low tide, song thrushes steal winkles from the wrack and break them against the rocks. Rock pipits are common along the convoluted, rocky shorelines.

Secluded sea lochs have breeding eiders: families potter about in the sea weedy bays, drakes loaf in groups farther offshore. Red-breasted mergansers nest in rough shoreline grass and fish in the clear bays.

Rolling, rocky and grassy hills are typical hunting terrain for buzzards, kestrels and golden eagles. Isolated islands with tall pines sometimes attract ospreys.

Eider

Buzzard

A northern firth

Large, sheltered indentations of north-western coasts of Britain and Scandinavia are among the cream of European bird habitats, with splendid headlands, soft estuaries and sweeping, shallow sandy bays.

Watch for ducks rising and falling on swell or flying low over sea far offshore. Look for scoter flocks and wait for white patches to show if a velvet flaps its wings.

Great northern diver, winter

Velvet scoter

winter male

female

Shallow sandy bays are ideal for great northern divers in winter; a few non-breeders in summer. Flocks of sea ducks feed here: long-tailed ducks, eiders, mergansers, common and velvet scoters.

Long-tailed duck

Common scoter

A sandy beach usually has sanderlings, early autumn to late spring. Other waders, including dunlins, drop in. The strand line offers food for snow buntings and (rare) shore larks.

Sanderling, winter

Sandwich tern

spring

Rolling dunes often have grey partridges. Shelducks nest in burrows in dunes and feed on wet beach. Sandwich tern colonies are erratic, often on extensive dunes.

Headland perfect for passing terns, gannets, skuas, shearwaters, fulmars. Choose a wild day with a strong onshore wind to bring the birds in.

Gannet

Marram grass on dunes holds few birds – nesting shelducks, meadow pipits, skylarks. But explore for migrants in autumn: these may include goldcrests, redstarts, pied flycatchers, wheatears.

Shelduck

Northern seabird cliff

The old, resistant rocks of north-western European coasts create sheer cliffs above cold seas rich in fish. Where the rock structure weathers away to create ledges or cavities, seabirds can find secure nest sites.

Fulmar

Fulmars prefer earth ledges near the cliff top, and fly very close along the cliff edges. Watch for passing shearwaters, skuas and gannets offshore.

Razorbill   *Black guillemot*   *Guillemot*

Gannets nest on the broadest ledges of sheer cliffs or over tops of islands; cormorants on wider ledges close to cliff tops and on stacks; shags prefer the deep cavities lower down.

PUFFIN

breeding and non-breeding

juvenile   *adult*

Adult puffin unmistakable in summer, but winter or young ones have face dark grey, bill smaller and dull.

The peregrine is a sea cliff predator. A white-tailed eagle may drift over. The golden eagle also nests on coasts. Great or Arctic skuas dash in to seize young birds from ledges.

Kittiwake

Peregrine

breeding

Herring gulls crowd on high ledges or in rocky hollows; isolated pairs of great black-backed gulls on prominent pinnacles, lessers on flatter ground above.

The sight and sound of busy seabird colonies is incomparable. They will be dominated by kittiwakes on ledges or dotted over the cliff face, quite low; guillemots populate narrow ledges running across the cliff.

Stock doves, rock doves (in the far north) or feral pigeons congregate on windy cliffs and in deep caves, often with jackdaws. Choughs much rarer, on wild cliffs backed by smooth turf.

Gannet

Razorbills prefer deep crevices. Puffins make burrows in grassy slopes or fans of debris. Kittiwakes often gather on low, wave-cut platforms beneath cliffs.

Black guillemots nest in boulder scree and rubble at the foot of a cliff or on sheltered offshore islands. Mixed groups of auks loaf on water under the shadow of cliffs.

Western headland and beach

The western extremities of mainland Europe and the British Isles have enviable beaches of clean, white sand and rocky headlands from which passing seabirds can be studied when the winds blow onshore, especially in autumn.

Turnstone

summer

juvenile

Purple sandpiper, winter

male

Black redstart

A steep rise at the top of the beach, with rough, broken ground and a few buildings, is frequently a territory for a wintering black redstart, also resident rock pipits.

Unless disturbed by walkers or riders, the local gulls use the beach for their long rest periods. Always check for rarities such as glaucous and Mediterranean gulls.

A bay of pure sand is likely to have more sanderlings than any other waders but dunlins, curlews and an occasional bar-tailed godwit might also turn up.

Sanderling, winter

Razorbills are more often close inshore than guillemots unless a storm has brought them into a sheltered bay.

Razorbill

winter

Guillemot

winter

winter

Red-throated diver

Where rocks, groynes or piers reach the sea, turnstones, redshanks and purple sandpipers are probable. Turnstones catch the eye, but purple sandpipers are unobtrusive.

A prominent headland is perfect for autumn birdwatching. Gales bring fulmars, shearwaters, petrels, gannets, skuas and gulls close inshore on some exciting days.

Watch for divers flying low and straight above the waves or swimming low in the water, backs almost awash. This, and their long dives, make them hard to spot: they rarely stay long on the surface.

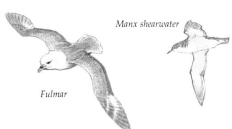

Manx shearwater

Fulmar

45

Baltic coast

The Baltic coasts of the north European plains have an unlikely mixture: northern and coastal birds plus some species most readily associated with southerly areas. The sea itself can be wonderfully rich.

immature

Aquatic warbler

Crane

Honey buzzards and occasional black storks inhabit mature woods inland. Goshawks watch over the clearings and hobbies move out to hunt over farmland.

Wetland areas still have garganeys, gadwalls, ferruginous ducks, greylag geese and occasional cranes, bitterns, black and white storks, (declining) aquatic warblers.

Ospreys and white-tailed eagles may be expected. Red and black kites and buzzards are all likely along the coastal belt.

Osprey

White-tailed eagle

RUFF

nuptial male

juvenile

winter

Female and young ruffs confusing, but legs usually olive or yellowish, bill quite stout and fairly short, on small round head; juveniles bright buff, clearly marked black. Males very variable; once ruff is lost in summer, head often white, bill and legs red or pink.

Caspian tern

Long-tailed duck

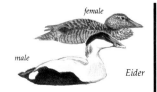

Eider

Shoreline reserves have breeding avocets on muddy lagoons, ruffs and redshanks in wet meadows and little, Sandwich and Caspian terns on shingle banks, islands.

On the sea in autumn and spring (often frozen out in winter) are vast flocks of eiders, common and velvet scoters, long-tailed ducks, mergansers and smews.

Dunes, links and sandy beach

Shorelines along the Atlantic, North Sea and Baltic seaboards, where sand dunes, rocky outcrops and extensive inter-tidal mud and sand flats come together, are especially interesting for coastline birds. Enriched by the tides, the estuary is a unique habitat of immense value.

Sand dunes have skylarks and pipits, but rather few other birds. Patches of woodland should be explored in autumn for incoming migrants, resting after overnight flights.

Skylark

Brent goose

winter

Sanderling

Look for sanderlings and ringed plovers on the sandy beach. Hard, slippery outcrops on the upper beach provide feeding for turnstones and curlews as well as dunlins, purple sandpipers.

Dry sand, shells and shingle are ideal for nesting ringed plovers and little terns; sometimes Arctic terns.

Winding creeks are used by eiders, shelducks and in winter a variety of grebes, long-tailed ducks, red-breasted mergansers, maybe divers as the tide flows in.

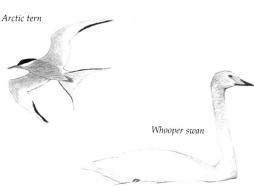

Arctic tern

Whooper swan

Flocks of greylag geese, wigeon and whooper swans feed on pasture and saltmarsh. Hen harriers and merlins hunt along the upper beach and marsh.

Ringed plover, adult

Long-tailed duck

Wigeon

Little tern

juvenile

Brent geese will feed on the wet, lower beach at low tide, or will ride the water as the tide comes in.

Estuary and coastal development

Many estuaries have industry, docks, bridges and urban development adjacent to areas of international importance for birds. Some species thrive in the varied habitats created here, while others decline in the face of disturbance.

Goldeneye
male

Cormorant

Barn owl

Look around sewage outflows, piers, bridge supports and other features where the tide may stir up food for foraging gulls and, in winter, occasional cormorants and red-throated divers.

Estuary mud at low tide is used by feeding waders and gulls; watch for dunlins, redshanks, oystercatchers and black-headed gulls. Numbers will decline if there is no safe high-tide roost nearby.

Rough grassland provides good hunting for barn owls, kestrels, perhaps merlins in autumn and winter.

BLACK-HEADED GULL

summer and winter

winter

summer

The black-headed gull really has a dark brown hood, then only in breeding plumage. Winter/immature birds have white head with black ear spot: look also for the white flash on front of wing.

Tideline and embankments attract snow buntings, skylarks, sometimes shore larks, rock pipits and assorted finches in winter. Thistles, teasels and yellow-horned poppies bring in goldfinches to feed on the seeds.

Pochard

male

Borrow-pits, clay pits or gravel diggings close to the coast serve as wildfowl and wader roosts at high tide, and add possibilities of pochards, tufted ducks, goldeneyes and (rare) smews or scarce grebes in winter.

Tufted duck

male

Skylark

In autumn such pits can be excellent for migrant ruffs, greenshanks, green sandpipers and other waders, as well as black and common terns and little gulls.

Ruff

juvenile

51

Coastal migration route, autumn

Autumn is an exciting season, with bird populations augmented by a new crop of inexperienced youngsters and mass migrations underway. Almost anything can turn up anywhere, especially on those coasts which birds will follow on their way south.

Great grey shrikes hunt small migrants, voles and beetles. Fieldfares and redwings are often obvious. Blackbirds and song thrushes may have crossed the sea too.

Barred warbler, adult

Wryneck

Clumps of willows on the dunes can hold exciting birds in autumn – wryneck, barred warbler, bluethroat and yellow-browed warblers are worth searching for after easterly winds.

Tired meadow and tree pipits pause in the marram grass or feed on more open spaces; whinchats, wheatears and redstarts rest in similar places, often perching on fences.

Small pools in dunes or behind the beach hold waders for short periods: watch regularly for quick visits by snipe, wood and green sandpipers, ruffs, little stints.

Muddy edges to brackish pools are likely spots for yellow and pied wagtails, migrant rock pipits, linnets, reed buntings and sometimes (rare) shore larks; and also Lapland buntings.

Rock pipit

Great grey shrike, adult

Fieldfare

Coastal pines and associated elders, blackberries and sea buckthorn give welcome food and shelter to all kinds of migrants, from goldcrests to bramblings and crossbills.

Redstart, male

High spot for migrants, Britain

The coasts of Britain and Ireland are exceptional for the remarkable variety of migrant birds that appear every autumn. On the fringe of continental Europe, they are visited by waifs from every direction. The best areas tend to be prominent headlands, or bulges in coastlines, which are the first areas of land reached by tired migrants after an exhausting sea crossing.

Pied flycatcher

female

Barred warbler

immature

adult

Icterine warbler

A mixture of estuary, sand dunes, beach and woodland guarantees excitement in autumn. The estuary will be full of waders and gulls, the open sea cruised by skuas.

Sand dunes used by nesting terns, shelducks, pipits and skylarks are now likely places for migrants, from young dotterels to pied flycatchers, wheatears and Richard's pipits.

Richard's pipit

Barred warblers, wrynecks, red-breasted flycatchers, bluethroats and icterine warblers are sought by birdwatchers in the autumn; dreams of Siberian rarities add spice to your birdwatching.

Visible migration includes thousands of starlings reaching the coast by day. Tired long-eared and short-eared owls come in off the sea to join woodcocks already in the dunes and coastal woodland.

Fieldfare

Sea buckthorn, blackberry and wild privet fruits are eagerly eaten by hungry blackbirds, song thrushes, redwings and fieldfares after long flights across the sea.

Patches of willow provide shelter for exhausted goldcrests, willow warblers, chiffchaffs, spotted flycatchers and rare visitors such as yellow-browed and greenish warblers.

Goldcrest

Redwing

Scilly: a migration honeypot

The compact, varied and close-knit landscapes of the Isles of Scilly create wonderfully rich bird habitats all year. They also serve as a mecca for birdwatchers looking for rarities, particularly in autumn.

Golden plover, winter

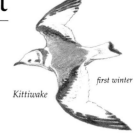

Kittiwake

first winter

Shag

The shallow channels between islands are used by huge flocks of feeding shags and small numbers of common terns. Kittiwakes often take refuge here in storms.

Outcrops of granite near the shore make the change in topography appreciated by wrens; rock pipits breed in and around them. Purple sandpipers pick about the rocky shores.

Purple sandpiper, winter

Autumn migrants include a wide range of exciting vagrants such as yellow-browed warblers, tawny pipits, red-breasted flycatchers, firecrests, buff-breasted sandpipers and American golden plovers.

Tawny pipit

adult

immature

immature

Red-breasted flycatcher

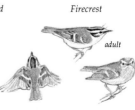

Firecrest

adult

Pasture and golf courses attract pipits, wagtails and waders of dry ground such as golden plovers, as well as their fair share of rare birds every autumn.

Tall, thick hedges shelter crops and make perfect territory for wrens, robins, dunnocks and song thrushes. In autumn they will hold almost any small bird from time to time.

Smooth sand beaches are excellent for sanderlings while the strandline is explored by turnstones, dunlins, curlews and ringed plovers. The plovers also nest here.

Ringed plover

Turnstone

summer

juvenile

Chalk cliffs and rough grazing

The chalk cliffs of the English Channel have a special appeal despite the demise of their once-thriving seabird colonies.

Hoopoe

Feral pigeon

Corn bunting

Watch migrants following the coast in autumn – straggling flocks of swallows, bunches of linnets and chaffinches, snaky lines of starlings, even a kestrel or hobby.

Wild rock doves are now found only on north Scotland and Scandinavian coasts, but domestic pigeons gone wild are abundant. The most likely falcon is the kestrel, hunting above the cliff top.

The chalky fields just inland are good for red-legged partridges and skylarks; also corn buntings.

Kestrel

Red-legged partridge

KITTIWAKE

adult and juvenile

adult

first winter

breeding

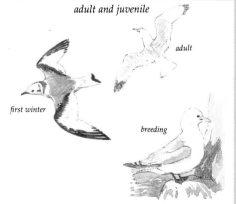

Adult kittiwake immaculate in summer, grey-hooded in winter; note juvenile has striking black zigzag across wings.

Incoming migrants (spring) include wheatears on the short grass, pipits in the rougher spots and swallows flying low over the cliff. Look out for oddballs, such as hoopoes (rare).

winter   *adult*

Pomarine skua

Arctic skua, pale

In spring, look for offshore movements of Arctic and pomarine skuas. Scoters, divers, bar-tailed godwits and other waders can pass by in considerable numbers.

Herring gulls are common, fulmars and kittiwakes restricted to a few colonies.

Some Channel cliffs used to have colonies of guillemots and razorbills, but few remain. Peregrines disappeared in the pesticide era and have been slow to return.

Rocky headland with scrub

Western headlands are windswept and exposed, and all the more dramatic for that. Their birds are typical of rocky shores, but have an extra element – those driven inshore by westerly winds.

Leach's petrel

Fulmar

Cormorant

Shag

Common scoters flock on shallow bays with sandy bottoms from late summer into winter. Watch for divers, eiders, cormorants, shags.

Keep an eye out for little owls on the rocky slopes. They nest in cavities in the rocks but often sit out in the open in the daytime.

Little owl

Herring gulls nest on most rocky coasts. House martins will nest on cliffs and (rare) swifts may do so in narrow cavities.

Herring gull

The low, wave-cut platform at the foot of the cliff is an ideal site for waders, especially turnstones, purple sandpipers, curlews and oystercatchers.

Chough

Ravens nest on some western cliffs. Jackdaws are more common, choughs much rarer and localized, rock doves restricted to the far north (but feral pigeons abundant).

The headland is ideal for watching birds go by over the sea. Look for gannets, fulmars, shearwaters, terns and auks – and, if there is a stiff onshore wind, you might see storm and Leach's petrels.

Gorse and rough ground above the cliff have stonechats all year, linnets and yellowhammers in summer. Wheatears pause along the clifftops in spring and sometimes nest.

Linnet

spring male   female

Stonechat

Coastal reserve: lagoons and islands

*Coastal habitats managed by conservationists
are among the finest places for wild birds in
Europe. Man-made lagoons in marshy places
are rich in food for a wide variety of birds.*

Gadwall

male

Common tern

juvenile

In eastern England and lowland Europe
isolated thickets surrounded by rabbit-
cropped turf will often hold pairs of
nightingales.

Watch over the reeds in spring, the best
chance to see a bittern. Very rarely, you
may be lucky enough to see one fishing an
open ditch at the edge of the reedbed.

Sandwich tern

Black-headed gull

summer

Teal, gadwalls, shovelers and mallards also
hide away in the wet reeds or beside the
deeper pools. Marsh harriers hunt over
lagoons, but nest within the reedbeds.

Shingle islands have breeding common
terns and black-headed gulls. The crested
black caps, extra-white bodies and black
bills of Sandwich terns help them stand out
in the crowd.

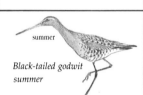

summer

Black-tailed godwit
summer

juvenile

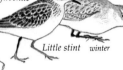

Little stint   *winter*

Grey herons tend to stay near the cover of
the reeds. The open lagoons and islands
are preferred by Canada and greylag geese,
shelducks, gadwalls, shovelers and gulls.

Curlew sandpiper, juvenile

summer

Ringed plovers nest on shingle and feed at
the water's edge or on drier mud. Dunlins,
curlew sandpipers, little stints, ruffs and
greenshanks are typical autumn migrants.

winter

Spotted redshank

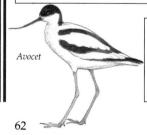

Avocet

Avocets nest on firm mud or stony banks
and feed in lagoons. The slightly deeper
water suits other long-legged waders, such
as black-tailed godwits and spotted
redshanks.

Coastal lagoon with shingle islands

Few places have such extensive shingle as the English Channel coast, where, in many places, enormous beaches and headlands have built up. Where the coast has been excavated, freshwater lagoons make exciting habitats for shoreline birds.

Moulting tufted ducks, mallards, pochards and other ducks in late summer mix with black-headed gulls, terns, lapwings, coots and geese.

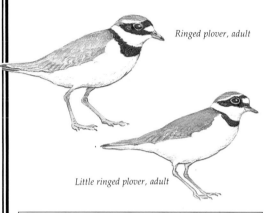

Ringed plover, adult

Little ringed plover, adult

Black-headed gull, summer

Great crested grebes are very much gravel pit birds these days. Watch for black terns in spring (when they are black) and autumn (generally dull grey and white).

Common tern

Roseate tern

Wherever weedy growth and bare earth come together, you should find linnets. Pied wagtails love stony ground beside water of any kind.

GREAT CRESTED GREBE

summer and winter

summer

winter

Great crested grebe has unmistakable ruff and crest in summer; in winter white-faced with thin black cap; long neck and breast gleam white.

Roseate terns (rare) may, with luck, be found with commoner species.

Shingle islands make excellent nesting places for common terns, ringed and little ringed plovers. Those with vegetation attract black-headed gulls, greylag and Canada geese.

Canada goose

Netherlands coast

The Netherlands and associated islands (the photograph was taken on Texel) are rich in birds, especially wetland and woodland species. In the Netherlands, despite drainage and intensive agriculture, wet pasture, reedy swamps and shallow seas together create superb places for birds.

The reedy pools in dunes have small colonies of spoonbills. Larger lagoons and muddy flats attract avocets year-round, but they are most numerous in summer.

Spoonbill

adult

Avocet

There will be great crested grebes and garganeys in summer; in autumn perhaps black-necked grebes, little gulls and black terns on migration.

Great crested grebe

In woods beside the dunes, look for short-toed treecreepers, coal and long-tailed tits, nuthatches and roosting long-eared owls.

Savi's warbler

Sedge warbler

In summer, look for bluethroats, reed and sedge warblers. Savi's warblers appreciate the reed and willow mixture.

Marsh harriers are common in summer, but rare in winter when martins, white-tailed eagles and rough-legged buzzards are rare but possible.

Hen harriers and short-eared owls fly low over reed beds and nearby dunes. Kestrels are common and sparrowhawks venture into open areas when hunting.

Marsh harrier

female

Stonechats are characteristic of bushy dunes all year round. Fieldfares, redwings and migrant warblers are likely in autumn.

Marsh and muddy creek

Shorelines of all kinds have a magical appeal. A beach, a rocky headland, a muddy estuary, even a creek with a small quay, are magnets to visiting birds, which enjoy the meeting of two contrasting environments.

As the tide comes in and fills the inlet, great crested, Slavonian and black-necked grebes may come in closer; cormorants are regular, eiders and mergansers possible.

Shelduck

female and brood

Pied wagtails explore the sea-front roads, quays and rocky embankments. The wilder spots in winter sometimes get a few snow buntings and, now and then, (rare) Lapland buntings.

Whimbrel

Curlew

Spring migration sees a short-lived passage of whimbrels. Common, Sandwich and little terns fish in the creek. Shelducks display and hold territories on the mud.

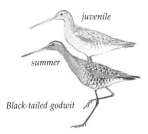

juvenile

summer

Black-tailed godwit

In summer, the muddy creek has redshanks, ringed plovers and black-headed gulls. Autumn brings curlews and oystercatchers, perhaps bar-tailed or black-tailed godwits as well.

Black-necked grebe

winter

Cormorant

The saltmarsh edge will attract rock pipits, especially in winter. In summer there will be reed buntings, skylarks and meadow pipits along the drier parts, too.

GT·YARMOUTH
YH447

Brent goose

Brent geese are remarkably tame in many places, feeding among the moored boats. Nearby will be herring, common and great black-backed gulls in the winter months.

Estuary: sandbar and stream

The best place on an estuary is the highest part of the beach, where waders and gulls gather when the tide rises. If there is a stream, too, they will come earlier to drink and bathe.

Dunlin

winter summer

Redshank

breeding

Little gull

Little tern

Cormorants line the water's edge to stand with half-open wings. Carrion crows can be numerous on drier beaches. In winter, the strand line attracts chaffinches, and snow buntings also.

Flocks of gulls rest on the mudflats as the tide rises, moving up the beach to concentrate on the higher sandbanks, or moving off to feed at rubbish tips inland, or at sewage outflows.

In spring and autumn, Mediterranean and little gulls, common, little and Sandwich terns add variety among the common, lesser black-backed, herring and black-headed gulls.

COMMON GULL

adult and immature

first winter

summer adult

Adult common gull like herring but smaller, darker grey above, bill greener, legs green not pink, eyes dark; note immature has brown wings, sharp black band on tail.

Close-packed flocks are often mostly dunlins, but sanderlings and knots may mix in at the edges. Clumps of invading spartina grass make sheltered spots for redshanks to take cover.

summer

Bar-tailed godwit

Look on the water for great crested and Slavonian grebes, occasional divers, eiders and scoters.

summer

Mediterranean gull

summer

juvenile

Knot

Sandbars uncovered except by the higher tides make secluded roosts. Oystercatchers form dense, uniform flocks; curlews and bar-tailed godwits mix; grey plovers will stand apart.

Muddy estuary

Western Europe is especially rich in estuaries and many have dissected saltmarsh above mud and sand flats. They are among the finest bird habitats of all, but getting a worthwhile view tends to be difficult.

Wide open mudflats are vital for knots, bar-tailed godwits, dunlins and grey plovers, which move to the marsh in order to roost. In the winter, rock pipits live in the sheltered creeks.

Small birds attract sparrowhawks, and merlins. Kestrels and peregrines sometimes hunt the marsh.

GODWITS

Black-tailed godwit

winter

summer

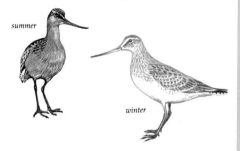

Bar-tailed godwit

summer

winter

Godwits are tall, brownish, straight-billed; black-tailed is longer-legged, plainer grey-brown, but striking in flight with broad white bands along wings; bar-tailed streaky brown, bill slightly upcurved, wings plain, white V on back.

winter

Merlin

Grey plover

summer

Gadwall
male

Shoveler

male

Smelly strand lines on the upper marsh are full of seeds and insects. Look for greenfinches, chaffinches, the odd brambling, reed buntings, linnets and possibly sparrows.

In winter, the swards are grazed by wigeon and mallards. Less often, gadwalls and shovelers are here too. Pintails are numerous on very few estuarine marshes.

Shallow pools on the upper marsh are used by migrating waders – look for ruffs, spotted redshanks, greenshanks, curlew sandpipers and little stints in autumn.

Expansive saltmarsh swards are full of dangerous creeks and runnels. Shelducks rest on the marsh, feed in wet muddy creeks, and nest in nearby areas of rough dunes and bramble.

Jack snipe

Greenshank,
juvenile

Coarse, calf-high grass in a squelchy spot makes the ideal habitat for jack snipe. Water rails may be driven out into the open by highest spring tides.

Estuary: saltmarsh and mudflat

Estuaries provide a network of feeding grounds for waders and wildfowl. On their remarkable migrations, and during the winter months, they need an abundance of food and freedom from disturbance.

Knot

summer

juvenile

Dunlin

Wet mud at low tide is packed with energy-rich food for dunlins, grey plovers, bar-tailed and black-tailed godwits, redshanks. Godwits and knots prefer open mud.

Grey plover

winter

Bar-tailed godwit

summer

juvenile

summer

The lower saltmarsh with creeks is grazed by flocks of wigeon. Brent geese feed on the mud at the marsh's edge. Deeper creeks frequently attract shovelers, mallards and pintails.

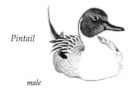

Pintail

male

Wigeon

The sea beyond a muddy beach and marsh can be interesting, or it can be empty. Look for brent geese, goldeneyes, eiders, mergansers and grebes.

Snow bunting, winter

Carrion crows are frequent visitors to beaches, poking about the strand line or among stones. Higher up, twites, shore larks and snow buntings are likely to come here in winter.

Herring gull

Common gull

first winter

Herring, common and black-headed gulls will be around in winter. Glaucous gulls are always possible in the winter months.

Estuary: pasture and marsh

Not all estuaries develop a flat, green saltmarsh. When closely grazed by sheep or ponies, the marsh produces a smooth sward laced with narrow, curling creeks.

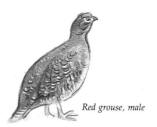
Red grouse, male

Moving uphill, there are whinchats, tree pipits and redstarts, then meadow pipits, skylarks, ring ouzels, red grouse, peregrines and merlins higher up.

Grey heron

You may see common and green sandpipers along the river's edge. Common sandpipers and greenshanks may stay all winter. Little egrets (rare) may appear too.

Kingfishers migrate locally, seeking milder conditions at the coast in winter. On the river, red-breasted mergansers are easily seen while grey herons fish in the shallows.

Redshank

This broad, wet marsh will have snipe and redshanks in summer, and flocks of wigeon in winter. White-fronted or barnacle geese may graze the nutritious grasses.

Curlews frequent the drier, rushy fields behind the saltmarsh.

Curlew

Wood warbler

Oakwoods near western coasts are wonderful in spring, full of redstarts, wood warblers and pied flycatchers. Buzzards display and call during summer.

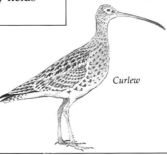

Snipe

male

European white-fronted goose

Redstart

Salt pans

*Around the shores of the Mediterranean,
shallow lagoons created or managed for the
making of salt offer habitats that are of great
importance in otherwise desiccated land.*

Short-toed larks are regular around salinas
in dry, sandy grassland or dunes. Where
the grass is longer, look and listen for fan-
tailed warbler song flights.

Black-winged stilts are common in and
around the shallow pans and avocets nest
on firm salt or mud nearby. Little egrets are
sometimes numerous too.

Short-toed lark

Black-winged stilt

male

female

The supreme bird of the salt pan is the
greater flamingo, which feeds in the many
shallow lakes of southern Spain and France
(a few in Greece).

Little egret

Black and whiskered terns, black-headed and little gulls are regular; in a few places in the extreme south both slender-billed and the rarer Audouin's gulls can be found.

Whiskered tern

male

Kentish plover

Crested larks frequent the bare sand and open ground and tawny pipits feed in the grassy surrounds. Yellow and pied (or white) wagtails are common migrants.

Kentish and little ringed plovers nest around the margins of the pans or along the network of embankments. In spring and autumn dunlins, little stints and curlew sandpipers appear.

immature

Tawny pipit

adult

Wetlands

Shallow water and marshes concentrate many species. Fish-eaters such as cormorants, **left**, and great crested grebes, **below**, nest near the water's edge. Rough, unkempt grassland provides hunting for birds of prey, such as the kestrel, **right**.

Flow Country

In the far north of Scotland a vast area of damp peatland, interlaced with shallow, dark pools, and now damaged beyond recall by forestry plantations, is a unique habitat known as the Flow Country.

Whinchat

If there are varied young plantations look for small birds such as meadow pipits, whinchats, stonechats and grasshopper warblers. Reed buntings concentrate in damp gullies.

A long watch from a concealed spot may reward you with interesting birds here. Hen harriers nest in young conifers in many places, but as the trees grow, they move on. Short-eared owls hunt the moor.

Short-eared owl

spring

Reed bunting

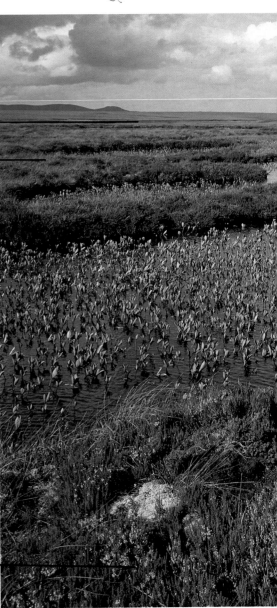

Patches of heather attract a pair or two of red grouse as well as bringing in an occasional black grouse to feed from nearby plantations.

Distant peaks will be the home of golden eagles and peregrines which also roam widely over this lower ground.

Wet flushes have breeding dunlins, snipe, curlews and greenshanks; drier parts may have golden plovers.

Greenshank, juvenile

Dunlin

winter

summer

juvenile

Arctic skua

pale

two types

dark

Arctic skuas add excitement in the wet flows. On the pools, look for red-throated divers, scoters and wigeon.

Coastal reed beds

Reed beds are scarce in Europe, but remarkably rich in birds. Most that survive are nature reserves – the rest are threatened with destruction. Their birds and other wildlife need better protection.

Marsh harriers hunt over more reed beds now than for many decades. Watch their dramatic displays in spring, and the acrobatic mid-air pass of food from the male to the female.

MARSH HARRIER
male and female

male *female*

Male and female marsh harriers very different: male brown with silver-grey and black patches on wings, female all dark brown except for cream on head and shoulders.

Small clearings in the reeds, or ditches, give the best chance of seeing bearded tits and bitterns. Bitterns prefer very wet reed beds with little accumulated leaf litter. Reed beds drying out lose their bitterns.

Bramble patches have dunnocks, robins and whitethroats. Reed warblers nest in reeds but feed in sallows; sedge warblers prefer a more mixed environment.

Reed warbler

Sedge warbler

In mainland Europe as opposed to Britain, add the following: bluethroats and Cetti's warblers singing from willow scrub; little bitterns and purple herons breeding in the reeds; look for spoonbills feeding in shallow lagoons.

Dense thickets of hawthorn and blackthorn need careful study – sit still, keep quiet and be patient and you might hear or see nightingales and grasshopper warblers.

Nightingale

Bittern

Bluethroat

white-spotted male

Bearded tit, female

Rough pasture near the sea

Agricultural land often blends into rough pasture and partially-neglected farmland alongside sea walls and old borrow-pits inside estuarine or open coastal habitat. This offers an interesting diversity of birds.

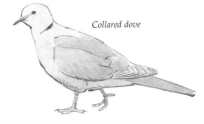

Collared dove

Shelter belts and copses around farms concentrate the few blue, great and coal tits, tawny and little owls, collared and stock doves, wrens, robins and dunnocks that live in this habitat.

Starling flocks are wide-ranging. Rooks feed on many fields within reach of their roosting woods. Carrion crows are usually absent, but pheasants are numerous.

Weedy field edges hold the interest of finch and sparrow flocks all winter and consequently bring in hunting merlins, kestrels, hen harriers and sparrowhawks.

Twite

Goldfinch, adult

Pheasant
adult male

Thistles, sowthistles and similar rough growth give much-needed shelter and food in these bleak surroundings for twites, linnets, goldfinches and yellowhammers.

Damp fields are grazed by wigeon, brent geese and, locally, white-fronted, pink-footed and barnacle geese. Introduced Canada, greylag and Egyptian geese may also appear.

Barn owl

Egyptian goose

Brent goose

Old barns, despite an absence of trees, may retain a few barn owls which hunt the rough grassland and saltmarsh edges. In autumn, short-eared owls arrive.

River approaching estuary

Many rivers in Britain and mainland Europe have been severely altered by improvements for drainage and flood defence, but the more natural they are, the better for birds.

Willow tits appreciate damp places near rivers, especially alder and willow thickets. A likely place for swallows to swoop down for a sip of water.

Willow and osier thickets, even a little way from the river, should have reed and sedge warblers and probably willow warblers.

Reed warbler

Yellowhammer, male

Willow tit

Look along fence lines for linnets, yellowhammers, whitethroats and wagtails. Migrants may include flycatchers, whinchats, wheatears.

male

female

Linnet

Little owls will move out from the willows, where they nest in cavities, to watch from fence posts at dusk.

Kingfishers make do by hovering if there are no perches. Grassy banks make likely spots for feeding yellow wagtails. Muddy stream sides attract migrant common and green sandpipers.

Kingfisher

Little grebe

Moorhen

Entrenched rivers are too enclosed and claustrophobic for wildfowl, but mallards and occasionally tufted ducks will nest. Moorhens will keep well hidden in bank-side cover.

Mallard

male

89

Lowland river, natural banks

A lowland river with natural banks offers rewarding birdwatching all year round. Wherever there are ancient oxbows and cut-off channels, clumps of willows and natural banks of shingle or mud, the range of birds to be seen will be most varied.

Chiffchaff

Grey heron

adult

Riverside trees are especially likely spots for treecreepers, willow tits, willow warblers and chiffchaffs, often blackcaps and garden warblers.

Look well ahead as you walk a river bank, as moorhens, grey herons, kingfishers and so on will spot you first and quickly disappear.

A fence post is the best perch for a kingfisher, rarely as conspicuous as people imagine, blending with the light and shade, shimmer and dazzle at the water's edge.

Moorhen

The likeliest ducks are mallards, but in winter tufteds and even odd goosanders may be seen. Little grebes are frequent.

Little grebe

Grey wagtails might be here in winter but this is too sluggish for them in summer – pied wagtails are more likely then.

Sedge warblers inhabit the long vegetation. Marsh warblers are excessively rare now, frequenting places with nettles and willowherb. Reed warblers only if there is abundant reed.

Marsh warbler, juvenile

Treecreeper

Kingfisher

Willow tit

Lowland lake or reservoir

While natural wetlands tend to be a declining habitat, new reservoirs have created some important environments for birds. Shallow, nutrient-rich lowland lakes are often the best.

In May, sanderlings move through in a rush, rarely staying long on reservoir shores. A stretch of late-summer mud acts as a magnet to lapwings, snipe, black-headed gulls.

Coot

Great crested grebe

summer

Ruff

winter

juvenile

Coots potter about almost anywhere, while moorhens stick closely to the shore. Great crested grebes are most common on shallow lakes and reservoirs, often out in the middle.

The shoreline is worth checking for waders in spring and autumn. Common sandpipers, dunlins, ringed plovers, ruffs and greenshanks are among the most likely that you will see.

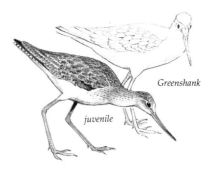

Greenshank

juvenile

Black tern

summer adult

Many reservoirs have common terns all summer; most have some on migration. Black terns are extremely erratic, usually passing through very quickly in spring.

Black-headed gull

summer

Autumn gales bring surprises – kittiwakes and skuas, for example. Kittiwakes also pass over, but rarely stay long, in March and April.

If the water falls in late summer and there is a good crop of weeds, watch for large flocks of linnets.

Pied wagtail

male

male

Yellow wagtail

Early spring migration usually starts with mixed groups of meadow pipits, pied wagtails and reed buntings on the shore; later yellow and white wagtails join them.

March and October are the months for migrant rock pipits, while in winter water pipits sometimes appear. Concrete banks often hold pied and yellow wagtails.

93

Wet pasture

Pasture that floods in winter and stays damp in summer is rare and declining, but rich in wildlife. Many species thrive on the soft ground, ditches and ponds and lush vegetation the habitat provides.

Snipe

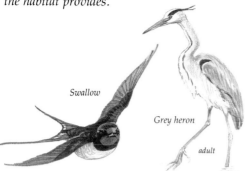

Swallow

Grey heron

adult

Grey herons stalk the edges of these ditches, looking for fish, frogs and water voles. In swampy fields snipe nest in long grass and probe for worms in the wet mud.

The flies around livestock bring in swallows, which usually feed at very low level, while house martins prefer to hunt insects higher up.

Yellow wagtails catch insects under the feet of cattle. Such damp, rough places provide the few remaining whinchat sites in lowland Britain. Barn owls may well feed here at night.

Yellow wagtail
male

Kingfisher

Moorhen

Despite one smooth bank, this ditch has enough cover to satisfy moorhens all year, and probably water rails in winter. A kingfisher could fish the clear water from a reed-stem perch.

Look carefully along the margin of the ditch for common sandpipers on migration and redshanks and green sandpipers in winter.

Reed warbler

Cetti's warbler

Where the reeds spread across the ditch, a pair of reed warblers will settle. In mainland Europe, even narrow lines of reeds can produce great reed warblers and Cetti's warblers.

Lowland floods

Flood meadows taking excess water from rivers make a special habitat which is very restricted in north-western Europe. They attract thousands of wildfowl and, if they are damp in summer, many breeding waders too.

Wide open washes can have big flocks of wigeon in winter. Pintails make for low, rushy banks and shallow pools. Teal often tuck themselves away under clumps of rushes or grass.

Pintail

Wigeon

male

Even quite sparse tree cover is enough to support the odd blackbird and mistle thrush through the winter. Wrens explore the low undergrowth beneath.

On deeper pools, look for mute swans, pochards and tufted ducks. The wet pasture and shallow flood pools are perfect for Bewick's and whooper swans in autumn and winter.

Bewick's swan

Whooper swan

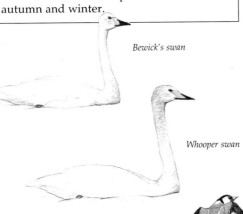

Goldfinch

Goldfinches are light and agile enough to feed on wispy seedheads. Linnets, redpolls and reed buntings have to feed on the ground itself.

Teal

Chaffinch
male

Short-eared owl

Seeds at edges of pools or icy puddles bring in chaffinches, greenfinches, tree sparrows and pied wagtails. Reedy fringes hide water rails, moorhens, snipe.

Short-eared owls perch or fly low when hunting, and roost in long grass. Bleak, grassy banks will be explored by small groups of fieldfares. Redwings move on in frosty weather.

Lapwing

juvenile

female

male

When surrounding fields are dry or frozen, low-lying pastures are full of lapwings, golden plovers and snipe. When these freeze, the birds move on.

Lowland pond or lagoon

*Shallow lagoons in sheltered valleys make
secluded harbours for winter wildfowl, being
less likely to freeze over than higher, more
exposed equivalents.*

Great grey shrike

Great grey shrikes can turn up almost
anywhere in winter, ideally preferring
scattered bushes and trees overlooking
likely places for prey, such as voles, beetles
and small birds.

male

Goldeneye

Whooper swans roost on quite small lakes
and feed on nearby fields if not disturbed.
Bleak, acid lakes with otherwise little to
offer attract a few goldeneyes in winter.

Rough grassland can teem with voles, and
this attracts short-eared owls and kestrels.
If there are no voles, then no predators.

Snipe

There will be little here in winter, though
perhaps muddy edges may bring in the
odd snipe or lapwing.

Kestrel

female

Whooper swan

Short-eared owl

99

Inland waters with reeds

Inland reed beds are rare and suffer from poor management or neglect. Where they are fed by fresh springs or streams, helping to keep them free of ice in winter, they provide welcome refuge for wetland species in harsh weather.

male

Pied wagtail
winter

In winter, the isolated bushes and reeds provide communal roost sites for large numbers of corn buntings, starlings and pied wagtails.

Grasshopper warblers give their 'reeling' songs from hidden perches, but may perch openly on a bush on warm, still, humid evenings. The buzz of a (rare) Savi's warbler is an exciting discovery.

Reed warbler

Pheasants often wander into reeds from surrounding woods. Mallards, shovelers, gadwalls and teal drop into hidden pools within the marsh.

Grumpy, repetitive reed warbler song comes from all over the reed beds, while the more varied, energetic sedge warblers sing from the bushes.

Bearded tits can be hard to find but sometimes fly over the reed tops with a fast, whirring action. Warm, still days in summer give the best chance of sightings.

Listen for the squeals of water rails and watch for one in a muddy ditch or other opening. A bittern may fly over the reeds; there is little hope of seeing one otherwise.

male

Swallow

Yellow wagtail

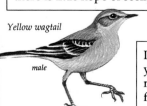

male

In autumn reed beds are used by starlings, yellow wagtails, swallows and sand martins, sometimes in large and spectacular flocks which come to roost in the reeds.

Water rail

Bittern

Bearded tit

male

female

Polderland reed swamp

Reed beds and associated marshland and lagoons provide good birdwatching at any time of the year, anywhere in Europe. Those around the reclaimed polderlands of the Netherlands are especially productive.

Bearded tits are common in the reeds.

Savi's warbler

In winter hen and marsh harriers and rough-legged buzzards are frequent. Buzzards and short-eared owls hunt around the fringe of the marshes and in nearby fields or grassy areas.

Extensive tracts of willow have big cormorant colonies and often grey herons nesting. Purple herons, spoonbills nest in the reeds. Bitterns are rare reed bed birds.

Rough-legged buzzard

Purple heron

Grey heron adult

In winter, the sheltered, reedy lakes are alive with huge numbers of tufted ducks and pochards; smews and goosanders can be numerous.

In the willows beside the reeds there are nesting bluethroats. Great reed, Savi's and Cetti's warblers are all possible as well as the commoner reed and sedge warblers.

Shallow lagoons are used by feeding avocets and spoonbills. Black terns are often numerous, especially in autumn, when the odd Caspian tern may fly in, too.

Black tern, summer adult

Greylag geese breed; in winter they are joined by white-fronted and bean geese and barnacle geese roost on some lakes after feeding on pastures with whooper and Bewick's swans.

Spoonbill, adult

Bittern

Avocet

Polderland meadow in spring

Old meadows and nature reserves on land reclaimed from the sea in the Dutch polders are particularly special examples of damp, lowland grassland. Unless protected for wildlife, they are improved for agriculture and lose their bird interest. The best are still beautiful and inspiring.

The dense woodland planted on the polders is excellent for golden orioles. In winter, it is full of buzzards, which move out to hunt across the meadows, using fences as perches.

juvenile

Lapwing

male

female

Black-tailed godwit

summer

nuptial male

Ruff

Golden oriole

male

Black-tailed godwits favour longer grass than lapwings, which need a clear view and less obstruction when they feed. Ruffs nest in long grass, but feed in wet and muddy spots.

The reedy ditches attract a few bluethroats and sedge warblers. Along bushy field edges and fences there may be red-backed shrikes, whitethroats and linnets.

Bluethroat, white-spotted male

male

Red-backed shrike

In winter the waders move on but white-fronted geese, wigeon and mallards graze the grass. Hen harriers float over the fields looking for voles and larks.

In spring many snipe drum overhead and call from posts or overhead cables. They feed where the ground is soft. Redshanks feed in wet spots and prefer long grass to nest in.

Redshank

White-fronted goose

Lapwings are still abundant where the land is wet. Drained fields soon become unsuitable for birds. By early summer lapwings move to pools and the edges of reservoirs.

Eastern European marshland

Natural marshes in wide, flooded valleys with meandering channels and choking reed swamps used to be common in eastern Europe, but most have been tamed by man. Some national parks retain the character of these ancient, wild landcapes.

The edges of the dense vegetation and muddy spots give the best chance to see the numerous water rails and spotted crakes. Little crakes often clamber about the base of the stems over water.

Little crake

Spotted crake

Water rail

Savi's warbler

Reeds and willow swamp hold an abundance of Savi's warblers; aquatic warblers prefer low sedges and mixed fen to pure reed, where reed warblers are more common. Sedge warblers sing from the willow thickets.

Open water attracts hundreds of black terns and some common terns: both species nest on floating vegetation and islands. Ducks include ferruginous (rare) and red-crested pochards.

Winter sees grey herons and bitterns forced into the open by ice, while the rails and crakes, breeding terns and warblers all move away. Excitement comes in the form of (rare) white-tailed eagles.

In spring the wet pastures and shallows are staging posts for many migrant waders, especially ruffs and redshanks.

summer adult

Black tern

Bittern

Little bittern

female

Reed and dense reed grass swamps remain excellent for bitterns, little bitterns, marsh harriers (in abundance) and bluethroats.

Ruffs breed in rough, wet grassland, as do a few cranes and corncrakes and many black-tailed godwits.

Inland flooded gravel pit

The loss of natural bird habitat to a gravel quarry may be offset, to some extent, if the pit is allowed to flood. Mature flooded pits make fine, secluded reserves for certain species.

male   Pochard

Big poplars and willows are likely spots for grey herons to nest. Sometimes one or two pairs nest unobtrusively for years, then the colony suddenly expands.

Cormorants may roost among the heron nests, their droppings killing branches or whole trees after several years.

Kingfisher

Enclosed, tree-lined pits are poor for waders, which prefer an all-round view. Kingfishers perch out of sight – listen for thè plop' as they dive in for fish.

Tufted ducks and pochards loaf about anywhere on the lake but often move well in under the trees if undisturbed.

Tufted duck

male

Chiffchaff

juvenile

Dense waterside vegetation has reed and sedge warblers in summer, reed buntings all year. Chiffchaffs seek early insect food in March, around the waterside willows.

Grey heron

Common terns dive for fish fry in summer. Where there are large insects or martins flying over a lake, a hobby might be expected from time to time.

Reed bunting

first spring

Great crested grebe, summer

Coots and great crested grebes build nests close in under the banks or in the shade of a tree growing from a small island. Moorhens will choose a branch dipping into the water.

Coot

Lowland lake, mainland Europe

Extensive reed beds attract marsh harriers and bitterns, but hard winter weather forces both to move out. Hen harriers hunt around the lakes and roost in the reeds in winter.

Hen harrier

Marsh harrier, female

male

female

Some of mainland Europe's lake systems, with extensive reed beds and flourishing forests, create remarkable birdwatching sites. Although interesting all year through, many are especially fine in the winter.

Crane

In a few special places, flocks of cranes come to winter in Europe.

White-tailed eagles are rare but regular winter visitors to some continental lakes and reed beds.

The woodland will hold black woodpeckers, crested tits and short-toed treecreepers. Black kites are increasing in some areas and appreciate water nearby.

Black kite

White-tailed eagle

Penduline tits are spreading west in Europe. In summer they nest in willows and poplars near water; in winter they resort to reed beds where they are often close to bearded tits.

Buzzards are common, red kites and, in winter, rough-legged buzzards much scarcer. Goshawks venture into the open, especially in winter, to hunt for pigeons and crows.

female

Rough-legged buzzard

Goshawk

Overgrown pool at woodland edge

Few waders use such overgrown pools as this, but a green sandpiper, snipe or jack snipe might be disturbed. Sit quietly and watch, as all are liable to be missed until they fly off.

Woodpigeons clatter across the treetops. Watch carefully for smaller, bluer, round-headed stock doves, often separating from the larger species in flight.

Jay

Jays are active in the autumn, collecting acorns; watch for them in the tops of big trees. This is the place for a sparrowhawk on the lookout for small birds.

Look for water rails on the edge of the water. In August and September, spotted crakes are possible, but very rare, at almost any overgrown pool with patches of mud.

Pheasants need dense cover and move stealthily through reeds and rushes. Overhanging perches are just right for kingfishers, but equally likely to be used by pied wagtails.

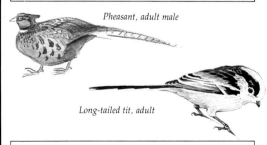

Pheasant, adult male

Long-tailed tit, adult

Roaming bands of long-tailed tits call as they trickle from bush to bush. Blue tits explore tall grasses and reedmace heads in search of insects and spiders.

Water rail, adult

Sparrowhawk

Kingfisher

Spotted crake

113

Upland valley with reservoir

A reservoir will often add to the attraction of a valley, although drowning many existing habitats for birds. Not all, though, are productive: it is the surroundings that support the wildlife.

Goldcrest

Goosander

male

female

Goldeneye

male

Fieldfare

Deep lakes and reservoirs tend to have few waterfowl, but great crested grebes, tufted ducks, goldeneyes and goosanders are all likely and grebes may stay to nest.

Redwing

Along the edges of woods and small fields, mistle thrushes will be in evidence at any time of year and in winter fieldfares and redwings arrive.

Look for old sparrowhawk nests – flattish platforms close to the trunk of a conifer. Sometimes a crossbill will perch right on the top of a larch or spruce.

male

Sparrowhawk

Sheltered areas in the forest clearings, and around houses, tempt late-staying house martins with young in the nest into September.

Buzzard

Goshawk

female

A glade between stands of big trees is typical goshawk habitat, but you need to be very lucky, or to sit and wait for hours, before you see one.

Big, dense conifer stands will always have goldcrests and, in some spots, firecrests.

Up on the open moors birds may be few and far between, but are worth seeing. Exciting birds of prey may include merlins and hen harriers.

A tall larch will often be used as a look-out by a buzzard, but don't expect it to be obvious – even near the top of the tree it sinks into obscurity, hunched in the foliage.

Woods and hedges in autumn are full of berries and seeds – woodpeckers, jays, woodpigeons, thrushes have a feast.

Lowlands & Semi-natural

Warm, dry landscapes with large open spaces are inhabited by red-legged partridges, **left,** while the few remaining traditional hay meadows and iris beds harbour corncrakes, **right.** Arable land has small birds such as yellowhammers, tree sparrows and corn buntings, **below, left to right.**

Rolling moor with cultivated valley

Many landscapes of western Europe and the western parts of Britain have pasture and tall hedges in the valleys, rising to open moorland or dry upland heath each side. It can be much softer than the steep ground with crags and screes on the edges of higher plateaux or on the low slopes of mountains, although it shares many of the birds.

Nightjar

In some upland plantations, nightjars can be surprisingly frequent. Unless you stay until dusk in midsummer, you will probably never see them.

In winter the fields are bleak and deserted, except for roaming flocks of fieldfares, a few blackbirds and chaffinches along the hedges, and foraging carrion crows.

Fieldfare

Red grouse

male

female

Clumpy heather on grassy slopes makes poor ground for red grouse, which prefer a more continuous heather cover, but there will be a few. Grey partridges may overlap on the lower, grassier slopes.

Magpies like the dense hedgerows and spinneys for nesting and search for insects along the field edges. Mistle thrushes enjoy the open ground for feeding, and isolated tall trees as nest sites and song posts.

Buzzards need trees lower down to nest in, hunting over open ground on the hill.

Buzzard

Magpie

Skylark

Mistle thrush

Skylarks are abundant on the windswept hills. Listen for them singing overhead and watch for feeding birds rising suddenly from the grass at your feet. Meadow pipits are often equally, or even more, numerous.

Dry lowland heath

Dry heath with heather on stony gravel and sand, often mixed with Scots pines and gorse, is fine for birds in summer, but a bleak, harsh environment in winter. A rare habitat in Europe, most lowland heath is in northern France, the Netherlands and England.

Woodcocks are best seen as they display at dusk, flying at tree-top level. Woodlarks sing through the night. Barn owls emerge to hunt the open heath.

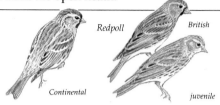

Redpoll

British

Continental

juvenile

Tree pipits are ground nesters and ground feeders, but use the trees as base for their song flights. Meadow pipits appear during their migration.

Redpolls fly over the heath with continual chattering calls and metallic trills. They are not easy to pin down, but often stop in tall pines or birch.

Old crows' nests in tall pines are hobby nest sites. Crossbills are unpredictable, but stands of pines are always worth a close look. Coal tits are likely in pine spinneys.

Nightjars love the mixture of open heath and scattered trees. Black grouse used to frequent this habitat in Britain and the Netherlands, but have retreated to moorland areas.

Stone curlew

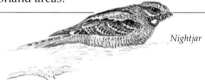

Nightjar

The bare patches should be examined for woodlarks and, much more common, linnets. Where the heath opens into clearer patches with stony ground, stone curlews may move in.

Dunnock

Tree pipit

Wren

Dartford warbler

Rolling heath with dense heather is Dartford warbler country. They quite often fly up into the pines. Dunnocks and wrens are surprise occupants of the deep heather.

Wet lowland heath and bog

Lowland heath becomes quaking sphagnum bog where it dips into valleys. Bog myrtle, willow and lily-covered pools are typical. The wetness adds to the variety of the bird population.

Hobby

Pools with rich aquatic growth have few diving ducks, but can be good for mallards, gadwalls and teals. Rushes and reeds make likely places for coots and little grebes to build their nests.

Teal

male

Dragonflies and swallows over the water attract hunting hobbies, which wheel around quite high and swoop down for their prey.

Jay

Moorhens nest near the bank, where an overhanging branch splays out into the water. Little grebes dive for small fish and insects, coming up underneath patches of water weed.

Little grebe

Thick tree cover overlooking a pool gives marauding crows and magpies a base. Jays and turtle doves prefer dense patches of woodland.

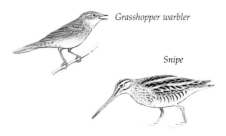

Grasshopper warbler

Snipe

Sedge growth on banks of pools and forest bogs is attractive to curlews, snipe and redshanks. Grasshopper warblers choose a small but obvious feature such as a bramble patch or hawthorn.

Curlew

Heath with bracken and conifers

Ancient heath is now often encroached upon by conifer plantations. Mature plantations with clearings created by wind-blown trees and selective felling are better for birds than the earlier thicket stage.

Mainland Europe's forests offer black woodpeckers, crested tits, short-toed treecreepers and goshawks. Honey buzzards feed in clearings but are often elusive in tall forest.

Great grey shrike

Black woodpecker

Scattered trees have tree pipits and willow warblers in summer; in winter look for great grey shrikes.

Where conifers have been blown over, the clearings are good for seeing mistle thrushes, crossbill families flying overhead, or hunting sparrowhawks or goshawks.

Goshawk

female

Carrion crow

Dense conifers attract flocks of crows, magpies and woodpigeons at dusk.

Goldcrests are often common in pine woods. Listen carefully for the song of the firecrest (much rarer). Woodcocks nest in these forests.

Goldcrest

Woodcock

Chaffinches are frequent and tame in coniferous forests, coming to picnic sites and lay-byes for crumbs and leftovers.

Nightjar

Open heath with bracken and heather is excellent for nightjars, whinchats and meadow pipits.

Unchanging farmland

The mild but exposed fringe of north-western Europe still retains old landscapes of small, stone-walled fields above rocky coasts. It provides welcome relief from the prairie landscapes of the east.

*Cirl bunting
male*

female

Swift

Coastal cliffs rarely have choughs unless there is open heath or traditional, close-cropped pasture where they can find plenty of ants to eat.

If there is stubble left through the winter, it is worth a careful look for mixed finch and bunting flocks. Cirl buntings need winter stubble to survive in south-west England.

Woodlarks occasionally congregate in ploughed or stubble fields in winter. Golden plovers and curlews feed in rough grass fields but are not found once pastures are improved.

Fruiting elder and hawthorn bushes along stone walls are excellent for whitethroats, blackcaps and garden warblers in late summer. Later, ring ouzels feed for a day or two only.

STONECHAT

male and female

female

male

Male stonechat contrastingly black, white and orange but beware female with paler chin, browner head, less white. Do not confuse with winchat.

126

Manx shearwater

Sooty shearwater *upper*

under *Chough*

Watch for passing gannets. In autumn storms, petrels and shearwaters are worth looking for, but you need patience and a sheltered spot to watch from.

Ants on the clifftop heath are taken by green woodpeckers.

Gannet

Dense, clumpy bushes on open slopes are favoured by stonechats. They survive the winters better on mild coasts than they do inland.

Deep gullies with bracken and gorse on the slopes and thickets in the bottom make useful cirl bunting sites. Look along the stone walls for perching wheatears, whinchats and stonechats.

Jackdaw

Wheatear

Swifts nest in old buildings where they can get access to cavities in the roof. Such buildings make fine starling nest sites.

Sheltered coastal valleys can hold exciting migrants in autumn. Open patches on bracken slopes often have linnets and yellowhammers. Jackdaws probe the turf.

Low-lying farmland

Wet coastal fields and marshy spots, crossed by reedy dykes, characterize the low-lying coasts of eastern England and the Low Countries. They are productive all year, but best in autumn and winter.

Willow tit

British

Marsh tit

Mixed woodland close to the coast and low-lying damp fields will be full of birds. Willow and marsh tits, blackcaps in the summer, redwings and fieldfares in the winter are all typical.

Woodpigeons appreciate the edges of woods with easy access to open fields. Wet fields are grazed by Canada and feral greylag geese; in winter wild white-fronted and pink-footed geese.

White-fronted goose

Pink-footed goose,

adult

Deeper open dykes are likely spots for wigeon, gadwalls, mallards and tufted ducks. Teal hide away in the reedy edges.

male

Teal

A marsh or Montagu's harrier (summer) or hen harrier (winter) will float over the reeds and ditches. Sparrowhawks will dash along hedges or reedy ditches to take small birds by surprise.

female

male

Montagu's harrier

Tufted duck

Rough grass at the water's edge will hold snipe and probably moorhens, sometimes a water rail or two. Sit patiently and watch. In summer, yellow wagtails.

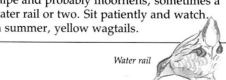

Water rail

Snipe

Farmland hedgerow

Bullfinch

Agricultural land has changed greatly in recent years. No longer are weedy stubbles left all winter, attracting big finch flocks. In many areas of intensive arable farming, the hedgerows have gone, too. New schemes for environmentally-friendly farming may bring changes for the better.

Bullfinches dive through the hedge when disturbed. Sparrowhawks hunt finch and sparrow flocks by flying along a hedge and then whipping through, or over the top, in an ambush.

Treecreepers, long-tailed and willow tits and even great spotted woodpeckers use hedges as through-routes on their wanderings between woods.

west European   *Long-tailed tit*

northern

Sparrowhawk

In the winter, hedges with berries make superb food stores for blackbirds, redwings and fieldfares.

Spotted flycatchers flit out of the shade of the hedge bottom to catch insects in the sunny spaces outside, but prefer places with a few tall trees, too.

Linnet

spring male   *female*

Corn bunting

Corn buntings sing from wires or from a stem of wheat or barley in the middle of a field. Linnets frequent the hedgerows, especially lower, thorny thickets.

Grey partridges are hard to see in a growing crop. They nest and often feed along hedge bottoms. A big, old, top-heavy hedge of blackthorn is best for spotting the lesser whitethroat.

Lesser whitethroat

Mistle thrush

Grey partridge

Mistle thrushes defend a berried bush against other birds in winter, obvious when one bush is still full of berries when the rest of the hedge is stripped.

Intensively farmed land

High-yield farming methods have destroyed many bird habitats, removing the essential variety of feeding and nesting sites. But there remain some opportunities for selected species in most places.

House sparrow

female

male

Where the fields sweep up on to the downs, skylarks take over. These chalky, rolling hills may offer (rare) stone-curlews. They are best found by listening at dusk.

Red-legged partridge

Red-legged and grey partridges feed in family groups over open fields. Red-legs do well in the more open dry spaces; greys need hedges and weedy field margins.

Yellow wagtail

male

Fields of rape tend to be birdless; yellow wagtails and even sedge warblers sometimes nest. Montagu's harriers (rare) settle in cereal fields.

Hedges between cereal fields are 'base' for large flocks of house sparrows in autumn. If the stubble is left into the winter, there will be large finch flocks.

Greenfinch spring male

Tree sparrow

male

Cirl bunting

female

Yellowhammers, house and tree sparrows mix with chaffinches, linnets and greenfinches, sometimes with collared doves, corn and reed buntings and, locally, cirl buntings too.

Hen harrier

female

In winter, an occasional stonechat may take up temporary residence in the bleak fields, and a passing merlin, hen harrier or short-eared owl may add excitement.

In late summer, turtle doves line wires above stubble, or feed in the fields. Dense hedges with a few trees make adequate nesting habitat. Collared doves visit from the farms.

Turtle dove

Mixed farmland

The mixture of crops and livestock creates such a cultivated environment – so free of wilderness in any form, be it rough grass, unkempt hedgerows or cornfield weeds – that bird life is all too often squeezed out. Any reduction in diversity means fewer species, in smaller numbers.

Common gull

first winter

Little owl

Lapwing

juvenile

female, male

Isolated large trees in hedges have few birds, being scarcely a substitute for woodland, but may be adequate for chaffinches, mistle thrushes, blackbirds and also robins.

Ploughed land is attractive to black-headed and common gulls, especially when newly-tilled earth offers a feast of earthworms.

Ploughed fields are worth a look even if, at first glance, they seem empty. Flocks of skylarks, with one or two meadow pipits, corn buntings and yellowhammers, are often there.

New barns can still hold little owls, but specially-provided boxes and much patience, plus some rough grassland, are needed if barn owls are to survive here.

Big, improved pastures are poor habitat for birds: foraging starlings, crows and magpies use them, but little else. Older, rougher meadows are much better.

Thicker, older, diverse hedges give linnets, whitethroats, long-tailed and willow tits, bullfinches and greenfinches a chance to survive in intensively farmed landscapes.

Lapwing flocks and especially golden plovers use traditional areas and even individual fields for many years, but they move around within sizeable winter territories.

Willow tit

winter adult

Black-headed gull

Skylark

Golden plover

winter

northern

southern

summer

Village and farmland: mid-Europe

All over western Europe, old-fashioned farmland is fast disappearing. This usually means loss of rough grassland, also of wet or damp meadows, with their farm ponds and ditches. This causes a sad loss of bird life. Where such places remain, typically in Central Europe, excellent birds are still clinging on.

Black redstart

female

Woodland birds include golden orioles, red-breasted flycatchers in damp spots, nightingales and icterine warblers, with wrynecks in sunny clearings.

Around the houses, black redstarts feed on roofs and nest in holes in walls. House martins nest under eaves and swifts inside the roofs.

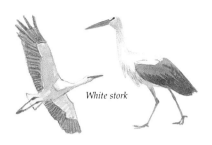

White stork

Song thrush

White storks nest on tall buildings, pylons and special posts provided for them. Only if there is also damp pasture nearby, and ditches with frogs or fish, do they survive.

Fieldfare

Red and black kites fly about towns and villages looking for scraps. Birds at bird tables may be raided by sparrowhawks.

Hobbies nest in clumps of tall trees. Montagu's harriers breed in large cereal fields.

Magpie

Rooks and carrion crows (hooded east from Denmark and Germany) forage in the pastures and harvested fields, often with starlings. In winter, redwings and fieldfares join them. Magpies are very common.

Lapwing

juvenile

male   female

Chaffinch, male

Lapwings and golden plovers flock on the fields after the breeding season. If meadows are wet, they are used by feeding snipe but they may have to resort to rougher ground nearby to nest.

Gardens on the edge of farmland are visited by chaffinches, tits and white wagtails. Blackbirds, song thrushes, and in central Europe fieldfares, are likely.

Snipe

Parkland

This habitat poses problems for many species. Ancient trees growing from a tidy grass sward are useful for some species but the lack of thick, natural undergrowth excludes many woodland birds.

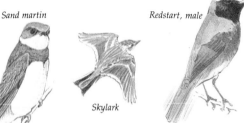

Nuthatch

Sand martin

Redstart, male

Skylark

Skylarks are typical of the open ground. If there are livestock and wet patches of ground, yellow wagtails may breed. Linnets forage over dry pastures in the late summer months.

Any large lake attracts sand martins, house martins, swallows and swifts, the latter sometimes swarming low over the water in thundery or windy weather.

Canada goose

Canada (and sometimes introduced greylag) geese feed beside ornamental lakes. They nest on islands or sheltered banks. Coots, great crested grebes and mallards are likely.

Restricted waterside vegetation tends to hold few birds, but sedge and even reed warblers move in if reed beds develop. Moorhens often nest here. Snipe and jack snipe are likely in winter.

Great tit

Jay

Iced-up lakes usually have a few ducks and coots looking sorry for themselves, frequently concentrated near swans which help to keep a small patch of water ice-free.

Stock dove

Hobbies are possible if there are spinneys of tall trees.

Mute swan

Mature oaks, limes and chestnuts are fine for feeding jays (which nest in denser woods nearby), and for nesting stock doves, nuthatches, great spotted woodpeckers and jackdaws.

Redstarts like old oaks and open spaces, but willow warblers and chiffchaffs will be scarce, both needing a dense ground layer for nesting. Blue and great tits cope well.

A town or city park with a lake

Urban parks with lakes are always full of common birds, many hand-tame if regularly fed. But there may be surprises here, too, if you stay alert.

Pied wagtail
winter male

Collared dove

Pied wagtails feed on pathways and along the water's edge when fewer people are about. Black-headed gulls are very common over park lakes from September to March.

BLACKBIRD

male, female and juvenile

male

female

Male blackbird spotlessly black with yellow bill, but female dark brown, young ones redder brown, often spotted darker on throat.

The short grass sward gives rich worm-hunting for blackbirds and song thrushes. Starlings look for cockchafer grubs in summer. Woodpigeons search for acorns. Collared doves pick up scraps.

Moorhens prefer the sheltered, secluded edges with plenty of cover and easy access to smooth grass. They rarely become tame.

Coot

Mallard
male

The ornamental ducks often attract wild mallards, tufted ducks and pochards. Coots like the open water, diving for food, or come to take bread.

140

Alders beside the lake have siskins, redpolls and goldfinches in winter. Watch for treecreepers feeding on the gnarled bark of older trees.

Woodpigeon

Tufted duck

Moorhen

Standard trees are excellent song perches for song thrushes and chaffinches. Rose beds are often visited by wrens, dunnocks and blackbirds; collared doves common.

Blackcaps and chiffchaffs are often the most likely warblers in park trees – follow up their spring songs to find them. Sand martins may swoop over the lake in spring.

Wasteland

*'Waste' ground, left after working gravel, or
as mining spoil, or the effects of building or
demolition, soon takes on a life of its own with
an abundance of seeding and fruiting plants,
insects and birds.*

female   *male*

Whitethroat

Goldfinch

juvenile   *adult*

Little ringed plovers nest on larger areas of
rough, open, bare ground.

Little ringed plover

Dense stands of nettles, brambles and
rosebay bring in whitethroats and, with
water near, sedge warblers. Redpolls
colonize mature wasteland bushes.

Linnet   *female*

spring male

Linnets delight in the seeds on the ground
under rosebay, wormwood and other
wasteland flowers; goldfinches feed on
thistle, hawkweed, teasel.

Pied wagtail

Robin

Pied wagtails are common among rough
ground litter with bits of concrete and old
metalwork. Grassy stretches may have
whinchats, rarely stonechats; even
wheatears call in at times.

Shrubs which thrive on disturbed ground – elder, hawthorn, bramble, buddleia – offer nest sites and food for robins, wrens, dunnocks, willow warblers, even for lesser whitethroats when the bushes are long-established.

Denser bushes in grassy spaces (but not on bare ground) are used by grasshopper warblers. In some places, nightingales occupy old damp thickets.

Willow warbler

Wren

A refuse tip

Refuse tips have rich pickings for birds, the most obvious of which are gulls, starlings and various crows – but a surprising variety find something to eat in man's rubbish.

Weedy places near the tip attract reed buntings, yellowhammers, linnets. In the evening, barn owls may arrive, looking for rats and mice.

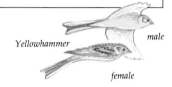

Herring gull

Great black-backed gull

Iceland gull

Yellowhammer

male

female

JUVENILE HERRING and LESSER BLACK-BACKED GULLS

Herring gull

adult

first winter

Lesser black-backed gull

adult

first winter

Juveniles are much alike: herring has paler patch behind bend of wing, paler tail, pale-based bill. Lesser black-back has double dark bar on darker wings, blacker bill.

Look for glaucous and Iceland gulls among herrings and black-backs in winter and spring. Black-headed gulls are the most agile, diving in as refuse is being tipped.

Pied wagtails are frequent in all kinds of man-made habitats: tips are no exception. Rarities on tips are usually gulls – Iceland, Mediterranean or even ring-billed.

Large, open, levelled areas are used by gulls for loafing between meals. Great black-backed gulls are increasingly frequent inland, dominating smaller species.

Rook

Landfill sites in old sand quarries often still have sand martin colonies.

Starling

Rooks gather on older parts of the tip, foraging for insects and grubs. Starlings seek insects on warm, compacted parts of the tip, often in large flocks.

The less disturbed perimeter of the landfill site will be used by feral pigeons, stock doves and even red-legged partridges. Kestrels hunt for voles, mice and beetles.

Urban/suburban garden/allotment

The density of shrubberies, hedges, lawns and patches of tilled ground make urban and suburban gardens particularly rich in birds. Many are of woodland origin, but live in greater numbers in these artificial surroundings.

Swallow

Blue tit

New houses are colonized by house martins but not swifts, which rely on old buildings with cavities under the eaves. Both feed high in the air; swallows feed low over open ground.

Nearby remnant woods act as nesting areas for blue tits which spill out into the gardens to find food. If there are old trees or hedges left, they bring thrushes, chaffinches.

Stretches of old hedge help whitethroats, blackcaps, great tits and greenfinches to survive. In winter they will be refuges for redwings, and the occasional surprise, such as a waxwing.

female

male

Whitethroat

Allotment sheds may even be used by nesting swallows, certainly robins and probably wrens and blackbirds. Linnets and even redpolls feed in the neglected, weedy strips.

Robin

Ground left bare during development will be visited by linnets and other finches looking for seeds. Skylarks may linger for a while if the area is left undisturbed.

Cultivated earth provides rich feeding for robins, song thrushes and blackbirds. Woodpigeons raid vegetable plots. Collared doves take spilled grain and other seeds.

Woodpigeon

Greenfinch
spring male

Redwing

House martin

Waxwing

Large garden or small town park

This is a typically English garden (or small town park) but many mainland-Europe equivalents share its density of cover for nesting, disturbed ground for foraging, and lawns, trees and berried bushes for feeding. Many different species find homes here.

Television aerials are used by blackbirds, starlings and collared doves during the day, and by tawny owls at night. House martins nest in mud 'cups', tucked tight in under the eaves.

Dunnock

Swift

Swifts' nests are hidden in the cavities beside rafters.

Song posts for robins, blackbirds and song thrushes are usually in the large, bare branches of deciduous trees and shrubs, where bullfinches may search for buds.

Robin

Blackbird

Dense ornamental conifers are poor feeding places but excellent cover for roosting birds and early nests, while many native shrubs are still in bud, not leafy enough for safety.

Tawny owl

Blue tit

Dunnocks shuffle about on disturbed earth, or along garden paths. Blue tits move from garden to garden, examining the deciduous shrubs but rarely the ornamental conifers.

Collared dove

Big conifers bring in goldcrests and make daytime roosts for tawny owls – listen for birds 'mobbing' the owls by day, and look for white droppings and large, oval, grey pellets to help you find them.

Song thrush

Overgrown, disused railway

Natural habitats have been so widely devastated by human development, whether by farming, roads or buildings, that the invasion of derelict or neglected ground by plants has a real value for birds.

Dense rosebay makes good sedge warbler and whitethroat habitat. The bigger bushes above are fine for lesser whitethroats and garden warblers, perhaps chiffchaffs.

Garden warbler

Whitethroat

female

male

Lesser whitethroat

Spotted flycatcher

Spotted flycatchers enjoy the shelter of a sunny cutting, but it is too enclosed for aerial insect feeders such as swallows.

Blackcap

Magpie

Magpies roam the length of the track and nest in the thickets. Jays are much more secretive, but also likely.

Where there are taller trees above the bushes, blackcaps move in, but if there are scattered bushes and more open, weedy spaces, willow warblers are more probable.

The old cutting of a disused railway is thickly grown over by trees, bushes, rosebay: all plants with prolific seeds which attract linnets, greenfinches, bullfinches.

Willow warbler

juvenile

Bullfinch, northern male

Woods

The mistle thrush, **above,** lives in and around woodland all year but the spotted flycatcher, **top,** migrates to Africa for the winter. Great tits, **right,** and great spotted woodpeckers, **opposite,** are typical, common birds of mixed woods.

Forest and bog, Scandinavia

Northern Scandinavia (including Finland) is a remarkable place for birds. Mysterious forests, lakes and bogs mingle in a vast wilderness. There are exciting species, requiring patience, and a little luck.

The forest holds black grouse, capercaillies, eagles, hawks, Ural and Tengmalm's owls, white-backed and three-toed woodpeckers, parrot crossbills and rustic buntings.

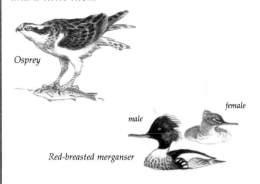

Osprey

female

male

Red-breasted merganser

In south-east Finland greenish and Blyth's reed warblers, red-breasted flycatchers and little gulls can be seen in the vicinity of swampy lakes and forest edge.

male

Goldeneye

Black-throated diver, summer

The lakes are not particularly rich in species, but black-throated divers, goosanders, red-breasted mergansers and goldeneyes make interesting watching.

male

Red-necked grebe, summer

Garganey

Beside larger lakes with extensive reeds there are marsh harriers, ospreys, red-necked, black-necked and great crested grebes. Garganeys and pochards are also to be expected.

Smew

male

female

Common and lesser black-backed gulls and common terns nest beside shallow Finnish lakes. Mallards, teals and, more rarely, wigeon and pintails also breed here.

Whooper swans, jack snipe, greenshanks, broad-billed sandpipers, some smews, and the occasional bean goose may be found on or around lakes in the north.

Whooper swan

Caledonian Scots pine forest

Scots pine is common over Europe, but in the far north-west remnants of ancient forests support unique bird communities. Plantations are far less rich than these beautiful woods, undergrown with colourful bilberry, juniper and heather.

High slopes are tundra-like, good for ptarmigan. Broad ridges above 2,500 feet (750 m) are likely dotterel sites. Red grouse, golden plovers and ring ouzels should be on the lower moors.

Dotterel, summer female

Ptarmigan, spring male

Magnificent, extensive valley forest: difficult for seeing birds. Watch for predators from a rise – sparrowhawk, buzzard, maybe golden eagle, osprey, even honey buzzard in Scandinavia.

Pines hold robins, great spotted woodpeckers, tree pipits, coal tits, treecreepers and chaffinches in abundance. Redstarts and wrynecks like old trees with holes to nest in.

Mixed forest ideal for mistle thrushes, which feed on fruiting rowans in late summer. Crested tits on the forest edge, sometimes smaller pines on heather.

Crested tit

Osprey

Mistle thrush

Low, boggy valleys have curlews, rarely greenshanks. Whinchats favour old, tall heather, juniper and broom.

Capercaillies take to clearings in autumn to feed on bilberries, which are also eaten by red and black grouse. Reds sit tight, black grouse and capers fly off at long range.

Capercaillie
male

male

Black grouse

Scottish crossbill

Old Scots pine visited by Scottish crossbills; they feed quietly, but fly off with loud calls. Siskins detected by squeaky, musical calls or quick, varied song from a pine.

Lowland deciduous woods

This is such a complex and intricate habitat that many species find a niche – there is no shortage of cover, food and nesting sites.

Pied flycatcher

spring male

Pied flycatchers take insects on the ground and pick food from leaves much more often than spotteds. Lesser spotted woodpeckers are elusive, keeping to the tree tops.

Rotting logs contain beetle larvae, weevils and ants, which bring great spotted and green woodpeckers to the ground; also great tits and nuthatches.

Jays are active in autumn, plucking acorns. Sparrowhawks are the predators of closed woodland, but you are most likely to catch sight of them outside the wood, above the canopy, or over open ground nearby.

Look for old woodpecker holes occupied by starlings – and fresh woodpecker holes.

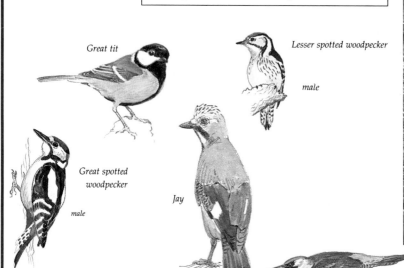

Great tit

Lesser spotted woodpecker

male

Great spotted woodpecker

male

Jay

Green woodpecker

Wood warbler

Blackbirds rake through the bluebells, looking for worms in the rich layer of rotting leaves. Wrens are abundant in old woods, mostly low in the herb layer.

Tree sparrow

Robin

Bright, sunny clearings provide the variety that adds tree sparrows, spotted flycatchers, chaffinches, robins, willow warblers and many other species to the woodland list.

Wood warblers nest on the ground, feed in the canopy and haunt open spaces beneath tall trees. A fallen branch makes a stairway between the tree tops and the leaf litter.

Woodland stream

The presence of a stream flowing through woods not only adds greatly to its attraction to birds but also gives useful open space and a focal point for the birdwatcher.

Large pines are sometimes used by nesting sparrowhawks, also (mainland Europe) by goshawks. Crossbills and siskins are increasingly frequent nesters in many places, too.

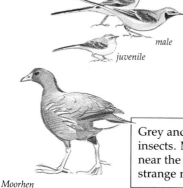

Grey wagtail

female

male

juvenile

Mallard

male

Moorhen

Grey and pied wagtails search the banks for insects. Mallards nest in growth of sedge near the stream and moorhens create strange nest sites, even high in bushes.

Streams in mainland European woods are the haunt of a very few black storks. Grey herons are more likely in Britain. Pied flycatchers nest in boxes along insect-rich stream sides.

Kingfishers may be found, but are hard to study in such closed surroundings. Birds using the stream to drink and bathe range from goldcrest to sparrowhawk or buzzard.

The woodland surroundings of this stream help dippers to do well in the clean, often turbulent water with plentiful stones and half-submerged logs.

Pied flycatcher, spring male

Both marsh and willow tits can be expected, although it is rare to find both in one spot.

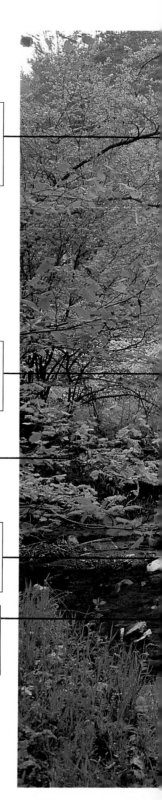

Sparrowhawk

Kingfisher

Dipper

161

Wooded pasture

Parkland and wooded pasture provide the sunny, open clearings close to safe, secluded cover that many birds, originally species of the natural woodland edge, can occupy.

Red kite

Red kites are found in continental parkland habitats and are being re-introduced into southern Britain. Honey buzzards are extremely rare birds of this environment.

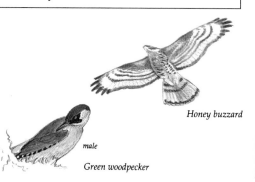

Honey buzzard

male

Green woodpecker

Green woodpeckers are equally at home on the ground and in the trees in this habitat, while lesser spotteds are also likely but much more elusive in the tree tops.

Tawny owl

Hoopoe

This is classic tawny owl habitat. Look for little owls where there are old or broken trees in more open spaces. Hoopoes nest in hollow trees in mainland Europe.

Great tit

This is typical starling, great tit, chaffinch, jay and jackdaw habitat. There may also be tree sparrows and nuthatches if mature trees are present.

Hobby

The fresh, clean air above open woodland and clearings is home to hobbies in summer. They hunt large flying insects and aerial birds such as house martins and sometimes even swifts.

Spotted flycatcher

Tall trees but little undergrowth is not the right mixture for warblers; however, chiffchaff and blackcap do best. Spotted flycatchers enjoy the woodland edge.

Old hunting forest

Honey buzzard

These retain a special character, with beautiful mature trees, plenty of young growth and sunny, sheltered glades in a natural pattern. The birds are correspondingly varied.

Jay

The predators of mature forest include goshawks, sparrowhawks, buzzards and honey buzzards, the latter rare in Britain but commoner, if secretive, in much of mainland Europe.

Old trees with craggy bark and much fallen, rotting timber attract all woodpeckers, nuthatches and treecreepers (in mainland Europe, often short-toed treecreeper).

female

Goshawk

Jays live throughout the forest and forage around its edges, where magpies thrive too. Carrion crows keep near the clearings or forest edge; rooks use the forest to roost.

Nuthatch

Hawfinches are present but elusive. Chaffinches are more abundant, and bullfinches are frequent in the sapling and shrub layer.

Treecreeper

REDSTART

male and female

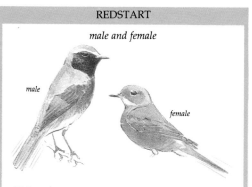

male

female

Male redstart unmistakably grey, black, white and rusty-orange, but female dull, with plain head: look for buff underparts, rusty tail.

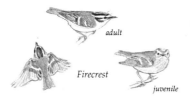

Firecrest — *adult*, *juvenile*

Firecrests breed in woods with field maple and spruce mixed through the oaks and beeches. Goldcrests are much commoner than firecrests in Britain. Chiffchaff is typical of mature forest.

A dawn chorus here would be led by a tremendous volume of blackbirds, song thrushes, robins and wrens, backed by woodpigeons, dunnocks, blackcaps, great tits and woodpecker calls.

Chiffchaff

Song thrush

Managed broad-leaved woodland

Woodland varies in its value to birds according to the way that it is managed. There are few European forests of primeval nature (Poland providing the best examples): most are affected to some extent by man. Here is an example of woodland managed by a conservation organization to provide the richest opportunities for birds.

A thin, open canopy is suitable for lesser spotted woodpeckers, while great spotteds stay on the bigger branches and greens often feed on the ground.

Tree sparrows find the clearings within a wood greatly to their liking. If the clearings are large enough, tree pipits move in too. Starlings thrive in such places.

Coppice (trees cut near ground level to produce many slim shoots or 'poles') with standards (trees allowed to grow tall and straight) means mature trees growing within an area of developing saplings and bushy scrub – perfect for nightingales.

YOUNG CUCKOOS

juvenile

adult

A young cuckoo is mottled and barred brown: do not confuse with bird of prey. Look for white spot on back of head; short bill opens to show large red mouth while giving wheezy food-begging calls.

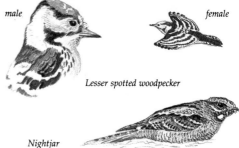

male   *female*

Lesser spotted woodpecker

Nightjar

Tawny owl

Warblers: expect both chiffchaff and blackcap.

Gathering dusk in summer would be the time to look for hobbies and later nightjars over the larger clearings, then tawny owls and, in a few places, possibly long-eared owls too.

Dense young growth from coppiced stems encourages wrens to nest. Later, coppice may become too dark and impenetrable for many species, except the nightingales.

Redpolls appreciate scrubby woods and bushy clearings and have become widespread in Britain. The typical finch in deciduous woods remains the chaffinch.

Tree pipit

Tree sparrow

Nightingale

Chiffchaff

Mixed plantation and clearings

Conifer plantations of varying age, with strips of beech at the edge and clear-felled areas, are much more attractive to birds than solid blocks of uniform trees.

In spring find a comfortable bank with an extensive view and watch sparrowhawks perform exciting displays. With luck, bigger, open pines may offer the rare and elusive goshawk.

Jay

Sparrowhawk

Inside the plantation will be a few coal tits, jays and woodpigeons. Carrion crows roost in the safety of the dense pines or in lines of beeches.

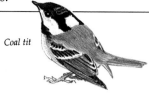

Coal tit

CHAFFINCH

male and female

male

female

Males are blue-headed only in spring and summer, otherwise duller; females quite drab, olive-grey, but broad white stripes on wings and sides of tail still catch the eye.

Young plantations may have whinchats, tree pipits, reed buntings and yellowhammers. Tree pipits like to sing from an isolated tree, or the clearing edge.

male **Siskin** *female*

Robin

Hawfinch, spring male

Crossbill, male

In winter, small finches flock in the pines and larches. Compact flocks and co-ordinated bounding movements usually mean redpolls and siskins. Identify them by their calls.

Hawfinches can survive along amenity plantings. Look along the pine tops for crossbills, which perch in the open before moving to feed quietly in the canopy.

Beneath the beeches, chaffinches, bramblings, nuthatches, and marsh and great tits feast on the mast. Edges of dense, dark plantations have robins and chaffinches.

Brambling

spring male

male

female

escape flight **Woodcock**

roding flight

On summer evenings, sit in the edge of the trees and look against the bright sky for nightjars and woodcocks; listen for grasshopper warblers in the plantation.

Breckland

In East Anglia, closely mirrored by a few parts of the Netherlands, there are extensive tracts of sandy, flinty ground once covered by dry heath and open grassland – the Brecks. Now largely forested, the old Breckland and its birds are hard to find.

Red-backed shrikes have disappeared from Britain, but lingered longest in the Brecks. Great grey shrikes still appear in winter as do occasional rough-legged buzzards.

A few curlews breed in the shallow valleys. Along the rivers, gadwalls are typical. On the open sandy brecks, ringed plovers may make their nests.

Sandy heaths used to have woodlarks, but these are now far more likely in the large, open felled areas within the forests.

Woodlark

Stone curlew

Stone-curlews nest on flinty fields and the ancient heaths and feed on disturbed ground. They need short vegetation cropped by rabbits. Wheatears nest in sandy warrens.

Nightjars are typical of the forest clearings and forest edge, where a few redstarts nest in ancient oaks.

Nightjar, female, male

Hawfinch, spring male

There are hawfinches in Breckland oakwoods. Bramblings stay late into spring in the birches. Look for sparrowhawks over the extensive conifer forests.

Crossbill, male

female

Siskin

male   *female*

Redpoll

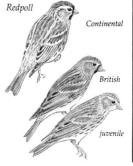

Continental

British

juvenile

Old, mature Scots pines can hold crossbills, but they are always erratic, linked with the cone crop. There are redpolls here, too, and frequent groups of siskins well into spring.

Wooded valley

Upland valleys with steep sides are often wooded with tangled old oaks, cherry and holly. Under the canopy will be a wide selection of shrubs and herbs, but grazing by sheep frequently gives an impoverished flora and therefore a wood that dies on its feet, with no saplings.

Tawny owls are common but rarely seen in such woods; few other owls are likely. Sparrowhawks are the daytime predators within the canopy.

Tawny owl

In late summer, the flycatchers disappear and birds seem few until a mixed flock of blue, great, marsh, coal and long-tailed tits, chiffchaffs, nuthatches and treecreepers starts to go by.

Coal tit

Hawfinches are sparse, difficult to find, but they do nest in tall woods on hillsides with beech, cherry and hornbeam. Chaffinches are common, and wrens are often abundant in woods.

Hawfinch, spring male

Redwings and fieldfares join local thrushes in winter, roosting in vast flocks in thick woods of sheltered, narrow, upland valleys.

Wren

Wood warblers and chiffchaffs prefer tall woods: look for the chiffchaffs where there are more shrubs and saplings below; wood warblers over open ground with leaf litter.

PIED FLYCATCHER

females and autumn

Wood warbler

female

spring male

Dense bracken or bramble beneath the trees hides woodcocks year-round. The open space between a dense canopy and the forest floor is exploited by pied flycatchers.

Beware female/autumn pied flycatchers: only summer males are black and white. Others have same pattern, but are dull brown and white or cream.

Woodcock

Mixed wood, mainland Europe

Mature woods of beech and pine have many birds in common across western Europe and much of Britain. Scotland lacks nuthatches, Ireland lacks tawny owls and woodpeckers. Continental Europe has several extra birds that are rare or absent in Britain.

Goshawks nest in mature trees but are secretive, although some are noisy at the nest in spring. Honey buzzards are summer visitors to the undisturbed parts of the forest.

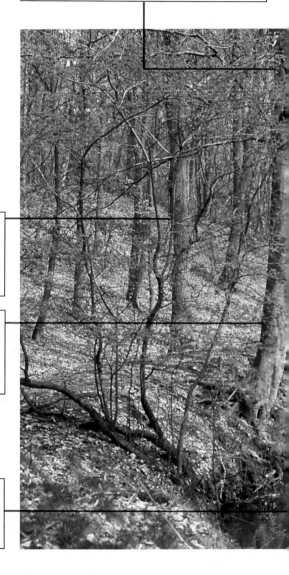

Treecreeper

There will be treecreepers in Britain, the Pyrenees and east and north of Denmark and the Alps. In the Netherlands, France and Spain there will be short-toed treecreepers.

Nuthatches are common and noisy in big beeches. Coal, marsh, willow, blue, great and long-tailed tits are everywhere. Pines beside glades are likely to have crested tits and firecrests.

Blue tit

Jackdaws are common, often nesting in old black woodpecker holes. Jays feed on the ground and fly into dense thickets out of sight if disturbed.

female

Goshawk

From southern Denmark eastwards, red-breasted and pied flycatchers nest in deciduous woods. Redstarts are much more widespread. Eastwards from France icterine warblers live in bushy places and clearings.

Jay

Large, flat-bottomed holes give away the presence of black woodpeckers. They may leave the woods to roam through suburbs and parks in winter. Their old holes are used by stock doves.

Black woodpecker

Marsh tit

Coal tit

Honey buzzard

Icterine warbler

typical adult

immature

Red-breasted flycatcher

Coastal Corsican pine wood

An open, mature pine forest is very different from the dense, dark thicket produced by commercial plantations. The sunny glades and consequent healthy undergrowth make it much more attractive to bird life.

Sparrowhawks nest in the pines and often hunt by flying low through the woodland rides or darting into bushes in clearings. They seem not to notice people if they are intent on prey.

Song thrush

Marsh tit

When the shrubs are in fruit, song thrushes and blackbirds are feeding everywhere, but mistle thrushes keep to taller trees or more open spaces. Fieldfares arrive in autumn.

Undergrowth of elder, hawthorn, bramble and privet brings in long-tailed, great and often both marsh and willow tits.
Goldcrests are common, especially in pines.

ROBIN

Summer juvenile

juvenile

adult

Only adult robins have red breasts: summer juveniles are spotted. Later they develop red patches.

Blackcap

male

female

Chaffinch

male

Common songbirds include robin, wren, chaffinch and dunnock. Coal tits like the pines and join mixed flocks in the autumn. Crossbills are erratic but always possible.

Willow warblers and blackcaps occupy the taller deciduous shrubs. In autumn, these and other warblers feed in sycamores and elders before or during their migration to the south.

Treecreeper

Great spotted woodpecker, male

Great spotted is the only likely woodpecker in a pine forest, but green woodpeckers do visit the grassy glades to feed on ants. Treecreepers, nuthatches are common.

Olive groves and orchards

In southern France and Spain olive groves and orchards of walnuts and almonds are familiar sights. The olive is restricted to warm slopes close to the Mediterranean and in central Spain; certain bird species have a similar distribution.

Stonechats are common in stony fields beside olive groves. Wheatears and whinchats commonly pause here on spring migration. Melodious warblers sing from brambles, bushes and hedgerows.

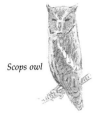

Scops owl

Black kite

Scops owls hide away by day in the old trees, emerging at dusk to call repeatedly. Little owls are more visible by day, often on old stone walls or barn roofs. Barn owls usually remain well hidden deep inside ancient barns.

Goldfinch
adult

Olives attract orphean warblers, goldfinches, serins and sometimes hawfinches if there are other trees, such as evergreen oaks, nearby. Hoopoes and cirl buntings frequently feed on bare ground in the shade of the orchards.

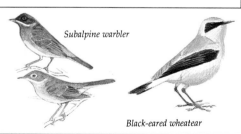

Subalpine warbler

Black-eared wheatear

The subalpine warbler and black-eared wheatear have the same distribution as the olive. Subalpine warblers like dense scrub, the Mediterranean *maquis*; black-eared wheatears prefer more open, stony ground, the *garrigue*.

Woodchat shrike

Sparrowhawks, buzzards and red and black kites hunt the olive groves. Short-toed eagles hover over open slopes and in Spain Egyptian vultures look for scraps. Woodchat shrikes perch conspicuously at the edges of orchards.

Nightingale

Magpies can be abundant in southern European landscapes with warm, open fields, sheltered orchards and belts of taller, denser trees. These may also have golden orioles from time to time.

Patches of *maquis*, with aromatic shrubs and evergreen bushes, are ideal for Sardinian and orphean warblers and nightingales.

Hill country & Uplands

Peregrines, **above**, breed on cliffs while merlins, **right,** choose ground sites or old nests in trees on moorland slopes. Red kites, **opposite**, nest in woods but hunt over open hills.

Valley farmland of the north-west

Agricultural land in the north and west of Europe (including the higher north and west of Britain and Ireland) often has a complex mixture of pasture, arable, hedgerows and woods beneath open moorland on surrounding hills – a richly varied environment.

Perfect buzzard country, with mixed woods, clearings, farmland, rough slopes. Heather above wooded slopes may have black grouse, which venture on to open fields in late winter.

Buzzard

Grey wagtail

female

male

juvenile

Pied wagtail

juvenile

male

Spotted flycatcher

Skylarks, rooks, pheasants on field.

Riverside shingle occupied by grey wagtails, pied wagtails, common sandpipers. In places, pied flycatchers take to riverside alders.

Valley wood full of small birds such as spotted flycatchers, chaffinches, willow warblers, treecreepers, long-tailed, coal, blue and great tits, thrushes, blackbirds.

Cleared slopes in forest useful for seeing sparrowhawks, buzzards, crossbills flying over open space. Scattered trees in rough grazing chosen as song posts by tree pipits.

Mistle thrush

Willow warbler

British

juvenile

Redpoll

Blue tit

Mistle thrushes find tall trees and open ground a tempting mixture all year round. Mistle and song thrushes, blackbirds and ring ouzels feast on ripening fruit.

Birches have a strong attraction for willow warblers and redpolls.

Rolling farmland

This landscape, found typically in the west of mainland Europe and in Britain, still has considerable variety. Gentle hills and close-knit features create both a strong visual appeal and a pleasing mixture of wildlife.

Skylark

Starling

Rolling moorland might have wheatears if it is stony enough, and certainly meadow pipits, skylarks in the more open spaces.

Hedges and trees bordering the moor is the mix needed by tree pipits. Lines of trees are used by treecreepers, woodpeckers and nuthatches moving between copses.

Starlings, magpies and jackdaws all look for ticks and other insects on and around sheep. Improved pasture has few birds other than occasional magpies, crows and also lapwings.

Buzzard

Rough fields attract buzzards. They stand on fence posts or the ground, looking for beetles, worms and voles.

Dense woodland with smooth edges gives little light for small birds, which prefer clearings or irregular boundaries where the sunshine and open air attract more insect life to feed on.

Swallows nest in farm buildings and feed low over fields with livestock. Starlings nest in barns or farmhouse roofs and fly off to feed in open fields.

Swallow

Open, varied woodland with light space is ideal for long-tailed tits, spotted flycatchers, garden warblers, willow warblers.

Garden warbler

Spotted flycatcher

Willow warbler

Sheep country, dry stone walls

In much of northern and western Europe, intensive agriculture is concentrated in the lowlands. The higher, colder, more exposed ground, with poorer soils, is given over to marginal activities. One can, however, find richer areas with rolling hills and mixed farming, with sheep and cattle in fertile fields, not on the open hill, and these are often good for birds.

Fieldfare

Starling

In autumn, fieldfares and redwings are common in wandering, restless flocks. Clumps of beech trees attract chaffinches and bramblings. Sparrowhawks are commonly seen using such small copses as a base for hunting forays over open ground.

The stone walls at this level may be used by nesting starlings, wrens and blackbirds (at higher levels, expect ring ouzels and wheatears). Buzzards and, in winter, merlins may use them as perches while looking for prey.

Yellowhammer, male

Wren

BRAMBLING

summer and winter

male

female

spring male

All bramblings have white rump (best seen in flight) and broad wing bars of orange (unlike olive rump and bars of white on similar chaffinch). Only summer male black-headed, but look for orange breast and yellow bill in winter.

Pied wagtails are likely around damp field corners, feeding troughs and in farmyards. Yellowhammers also benefit from spilled food stuffs in winter, when some reed buntings from the damper hills may come down to join them.

Lapwings nest in undisturbed, old pastures: in improved fields with sheep their nests are likely to be trampled. Carrion crows will perch in trees close by, waiting for their chance to take an egg if the lapwings are put up.

Lapwing, winter

Chaffinch, male

Jackdaw

Rook

Skylarks are common in such landscapes, singing in spring and again in autumn when larger flocks gather on the ploughed fields. Meadow pipits visit the fields in spring and autumn, before and after nesting in the hills.

Rooks are numerous, especially close to large copses and spinneys of mature trees where they nest. Jackdaws occupy old nests and cavities in large trees. In the fields the two feed together, frequently with lapwings and gulls.

Bracken, birch and pine

*Sandy hills with birches and pines
undergrown by bracken and rough grass can
be interesting for birds in spring, but almost
deserted in winter.*

This is the kind of place to keep an eye out
overhead – feeding swifts, swallows,
martins and dragonflies could well be
targets for hunting hobbies.

Tall trees are song posts and open ground
feeding and nesting places for tree pipits.
Even isolated pines are visited by crossbills
when there is a big crop of cones.

Willow warblers come to the birches in
spring. Redpolls bounce along above the
trees all winter. They feed in the birches, or
beneath them when the fallen seeds carpet
the ground.

Willow warbler

Tree pipit

The denser conifers make safe roosts for
many woodpigeons and a refuge for jays
(which tend to feed elsewhere). Pheasants
emerge to feed on the edges.

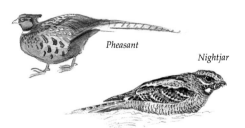

Pheasant

Nightjar

Birds feeding in the bracken include robin,
dunnock, wren and whinchat. If the
clearings are large enough, nightjars might
appear. At dusk, woodcocks will perform
curious display flights.

Hobby

Redpoll

Continental

British

juvenile

Jay

Wren

Chalkland

Chalk and limestone add a special element to a landscape and its vegetation. Such hillsides, with rough grazing and scrub, reflect this with a distinctive bird life.

Kestrels revel in the open, breezy airspace above the downs, although they nest lower down in old trees, quarries or barns. Buzzards are locally common.

Kestrel

Lesser whitethroat

In early summer the lesser whitethroat is likely to be heard in a dense woodland strip such as this. Song thrushes use hedges or scrub in limy places with plentiful snails.

Corn buntings spend long periods singing from wires or from the tops of hawthorns. Rough grassland with bramble and hawthorn is grasshopper warbler territory.

Grasshopper warbler

Corn bunting

Linnet   *female*

spring male

juvenile

This is a spot where wheatears, whinchats, thrushes, flycatchers and so on will be found from time to time on migration.

In late autumn, lapwings and golden plovers feed on undisturbed short grass. Fieldfares, redwings and starlings forage here; ring ouzels are rare spring migrants.

Yellowhammer and linnet are birds of chalkland scrub. Look for them on tops of small bushes and in short grass in the lee of thickets. Skylarks sing over windswept slopes (listen hard).

male

Skylark

Yellowhammer

Chalk down: woods and grassland

Nuthatches are common in big trees. Look for old woodpecker nest holes – green and great spotted, and also black in parts of mainland Europe. There may be woodpeckers, or starlings, stock doves or jackdaws in them.

Buzzards enjoy the updraughts above steep slopes; there may be ravens, too. Carrion crows are more widespread and often common unless persecuted: magpies too.

Nuthatch

Green woodpecker

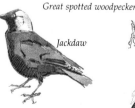

Jackdaw

Great spotted woodpecker

male

The hills of chalk and limestone in more temperate parts of Europe often develop a mixture of close-cropped grass (if there are sheep), overgrown, scrubby slopes where the grazing is reduced, and woods of beech, oak, ash and holly on the steeper slopes or beside clear streams.

Blackcap

male

Chiffchaff

Wood warbler

Dark woods with layers of fallen leaves beneath dense canopies are prime wood warbler habitat. Chiffchaffs and blackcaps also occupy these woods; garden warblers prefer the bushier, sunnier places.

Rooks, even grey herons, nest in the tops of valley-side woods, but fly away to feed in the lowlands. Look in these tall woods for shy hawfinches, often at the top of a tree, or flying fast along the wood's edge.

Hawfinch, spring male

Yellowhammer, male

Scrubby slopes with short grass tend to attract linnets, which feed on the ground, but nest in the bushes. Yellowhammers do much the same. On higher ground in France and Spain, look for ortolan buntings in the open areas.

Cirl buntings sing from bushy slopes in France but are no longer found in this habitat in Britain.

male *Cirl bunting*

Limestone hill and crag

Feral pigeon

Ring ouzel

Not all uplands are the same, even if physically close neighbours. Limestone always adds a different character, affecting the vegetation and land formation which, in turn, affect the birdlife.

Big, sheer limestone crags make fine nesting places for certain birds. You may see peregrines. More likely, there will be ravens, jackdaws, stock doves and feral pigeons to see.

Ring ouzels love the coarse screes of limestone hills. Drystone wall country, with close-cropped grass, is ideal for wheatears.

Wheatear, female

Ash trees often have pied flycatchers; they will usually hold chiffchaffs, willow warblers, nuthatches and spotted flycatchers.

Lapwings nest in these fields, but eggs and chicks face trampling by sheep.

Pied flycatcher, spring male

juvenile

female

Lapwing, male

Yellow wagtails like valley-bottom fields with sheep, cattle or horses, especially near wetter flushes or richly-vegetated ditches.

Yellow wagtail

female   *male*

A clean river is a dipper's dream.

Dipper

Northern uplands and lake

The highlands of Scotland are a unique and dramatic mixture of sharp peaks, crags, low moorland, pools and bogs. Birds are relatively sparse, but they are often exciting.

Look for golden eagles over distant peaks, high above buzzards. They are often just dots in the sky, moving in slow circles or long majestic glides. Peregrines leave crags to hunt over open ground.

Wigeon

Golden eagle

Red-throated diver, summer

Red-throated and black-throated divers on larger lochs; red-throated even on the small pools (*dubh lochans*). Rushy shallows may hold Slavonian grebes. Watch for wildfowl, too – teal, wigeon.

Whinchats, stonechats, meadow pipits on lower bracken or grassy slopes.

The water's edge attracts common sandpipers, greenshanks and (rare) wood sandpipers. In autumn and winter, whooper swans and goldeneye will be on the water.

Meadow pipit

Merlins nest on heathery knolls and use a rock or hummock as a look-out or plucking post, but are usually inconspicuous. Noise means the nest is close by, so move away.

Merlin

High stony slopes have ptarmigan, maybe golden plovers or dotterels. Lower slopes too bleak for most birds, but ring ouzels, wheatears, ravens, and hooded crows are often around.

Slavonian grebe

Steep-sided valley

In the hilly western fringe of north-western Europe there are many areas of upland where fertile valleys blend upwards through marginal farmland on to sheep walks and finally rolling heather moor. The birdwatching can be splendid.

Dipper

Buzzard

Raven

Peregrine

HEN HARRIER

male and female

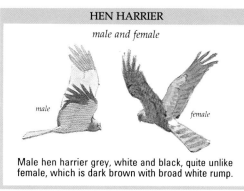

male

female

Male hen harrier grey, white and black, quite unlike female, which is dark brown with broad white rump.

The high sheep walk could retain a few golden plovers and curlews; wetter places have snipe and redshanks. Hen harriers and merlins nest up here, and red grouse live in the heather.

Crags above the valley slope make ideal peregrine, raven, buzzard and kestrel sites; ring ouzels, wheatears and stock doves nest there, too.

Tree pipit

Whinchat

Higher fields with scattered trees are typical tree pipit country; whinchats hang around the upper walls and hedgebanks, wheatears the open grass beside stone walls and scree.

Bushy slopes have crows, magpies, occasionally merlins and long-eared owls. A few redstarts, whinchats, tree and meadow pipits, and cuckoos; sometimes black grouse.

Riverside birds include dippers, common sandpipers and grey wagtails, pied flycatchers, treecreepers, nuthatches and garden warblers in the oaks and alders.

Cuckoo

Skylarks and meadow pipits common here. Swifts feed overhead, swallows keep to sheltered valleys. Mistle thrushes prefer the big trees low down, but also feed on moors.

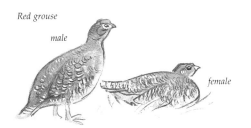

Red grouse

male

female

Common sandpiper
summer

199

Scrubby upland slope

Boulders provide look-outs and nest holes for wheatears. Little owls nest, too. Rocky tors are the likeliest spots for migrant or breeding ring ouzels.

Whinchat

Scattered hawthorns are perfect for whinchats, tree pipits, perhaps redstarts. Bracken has few birds: whinchats love it. The isolated larches attract black grouse, ravens, crows and crossbills.

Wheatear

Many coastal and upland areas of western Europe have heaths and moors on the higher ground, grading down into slopes of bracken, with larches and scrubby hawthorn.

Tree pipit

Moorland edge is skylark and meadow pipit country. In winter, fieldfares and redwings forage in nearby fields and use trees as refuges when disturbed.

The bracken, hawthorn and heather mix is so full of pipits that cuckoos also find it irresistible.

Cuckoo

juvenile

Carrion crow

Long-eared owl

Merlin

Older hawthorns attract crows which build big nests. Subsequently these are often taken over by merlins and sometimes by long-eared owls or kestrels.

Marginal upland farmland

Farmland varies immensely from place to place. The farmed land on the edges of the western and northern uplands of Europe is sometimes harsh, yet often varied enough to be both beautiful and interesting for birds and birdwatchers.

Trees along upper borders of farmland are typically used by tree pipits and redstarts, but many birds, including mistle thrush, chaffinch, cuckoo and spotted flycatcher, can also be seen.

Rough ground left between improved fields is good for grey partridges, possibly black grouse, and curlews and snipe if there is water lying.

Kestrels often nest in old barns, even close to villages. Woodpigeons occasionally find a safe place in the trees in a village or beside a farm.

Sparrowhawks, kestrels and buzzards are all possible in clumps of trees.

Pink-footed goose

Greylag goose

Low-lying pastures are visited by pink-footed and greylag geese in autumn and winter. They roost on the lake.

Rough fields are searched by mistle thrushes and, autumn to spring, redwings and fieldfares. Rooks are common.

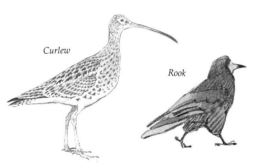

Curlew

Rook

Fields with sheep usually have starlings, and probably rooks, crows, jackdaws and magpies too.

Kestrel

female

Tree pipit

Grey partridge

Rolling upland heath

Semi-natural heather moor, maintained by cutting, grazing and burning is the classic habitat for grouse and other key upland species. Always explore local features such as incised streams, screes, crags and also patches of hawthorns.

Hen harrier, male

Newly-cut tracks attract wheatears, which feed on grassy places but nest among stones. Damper hollows and valleys have breeding curlews, snipes and redshanks in wettest parts.

Stonechat

Meadow pipit

Merlin

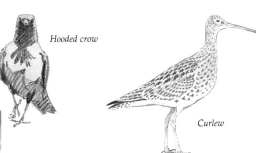

Hooded crow

Curlew

Open slopes attract flocks of young starlings and rooks in late summer, sometimes groups of adolescent ravens. Crows' nests in isolated bushes may be taken over by merlins.

Hen harriers hunt along rushy hollows and gullies. Merlins are elusive on heathery slopes – often found when noisily chasing crows out of territory.

male   Red grouse

female

Heather/conifer mix locally suitable for black grouse, short-eared owls. Meadow pipits common, attracting many cuckoos; also possible are merlins and marauding sparrowhawks.

Strips of tall heather give cover for nesting red grouse; watch males establishing territory in spring, calling from tall clumps and flying low over the moor.

Whinchat

Scattered conifers are used by wrens, dunnocks, meadow (sometimes tree) pipits. Whinchats and stonechats audible but hard to spot far away on bracken slopes.

Crag and slope, southern Europe

Although cold, bleak and often birdless in winter, rocky peaks and scrubby upland forest in France and around the Mediterranean becomes hot, sunny and full of life in summer. Spring sees a flurry of activity and bird-song, but the birds are often elusive by late summer.

In southern France and Spain scan the topmost pinnacles, or tiny ledges on the face of the cliff: suitable spots for blue rock thrushes, whose blackbird-like song will carry far.

female

Blue rock thrush

male

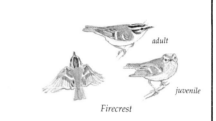

adult

juvenile

Firecrest

Black-eared wheatear

Crag martins float to and fro across the face of the cliff, catching insects in flight; house martins frequently nest low down under sheltered overhangs.

Black-eared wheatears like clearings with stony or rocky ground. Black wheatears are found in this kind of habitat only in Iberia and the extreme south of France. They frequently perch on the lower cliff face.

Woodchat shrike

The broom bushes should be checked for Sardinian and Dartford warblers, whitethroats and stonechats. Woodchat shrikes hang around the edges of open clearings.

The regular birds of prey on most crags are kestrels. Hobbies may hunt overhead but are not really birds of cliffs and peaks.

The low pines seem full of serins in spring; Bonelli's warblers, chiffchaffs, firecrests and short-toed treecreepers are common.

Kestrel

Hobby

Bonelli's warbler

Uplands, central or southern Europe

Red kite

In central southern France, the mountains of the Massif Central and the Cevennes offer a mixture of birds, both southern and Alpine species.

Black kite

Eagle owls are, sadly, very rare, but they do inhabit these upland areas with mixed wooded slopes, crags and gorges. Little owls are among the rocks, scops owls in the open woods in summer.

Wooded hillsides in places with warm sunny summers are ideal for both red and black kites. The more widely distributed buzzard is happy to live in these rich valleys, too.

Redstart

Golden eagles survive in remote parts and short-toed eagles nest in hillside woods and hunt over more open slopes, often hovering at great height before plunging on to an unsuspecting snake.

The mix of trees and rocks is good for redstarts (nightingales prefer deeper thickets in valleys, black redstarts the rockier places and village rooftops).

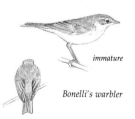

immature

Bonelli's warbler

Hot, rocky slopes with sparse vegetation are preferred by rock sparrows; linnets are common in high clearings and meadows.

Sparse, dry valley woods of oak, beech or pine are occupied by Bonelli's warblers (beware confusion of their song with that of cirl buntings).

Hoopoe

Ortolans sing from bushy, stony slopes in much the same places as cirl buntings and rock buntings. Hoopoes are frequent here.

Short-toed eagle

Cirl bunting

male

female

Rock bunting

male

Mountains

On most open, mountainous or upland areas, meadow pipits, **top,** are common. Red grouse, **right,** occupy high, open heather moors or upland heath, while golden eagles and ravens, **above,** forage widely over mountains where carrion is especially important to help them through the winter.

Mountain and valley, far north-west

In the north and west of Scotland and Scandinavia, high plateaux divided by dizzy cliffs, screes and deep corries provide all the elements important to mountain birds. The tops resemble Arctic tundra, but fall away to bird-rich moors and forests.

Meadow pipits common on heathery slopes. Skylarks reach surprising altitudes. Isolated pines visited by crossbills if cone crop is good.

Ring ouzel

Siskin
male

High slopes have flocks of snow buntings in winter. In summer look for them near snow fields. Gullies and folds of lower slopes have ring ouzels and merlins in summer months.

Snow bunting, winter

Broad heather-covered ridges ideal for nesting hen harriers, but merlins, kestrels, buzzards also hunt here.

Watch wet, rushy patches in valley bottom for snipe, maybe even teal.

CROSSBILLS
old and young

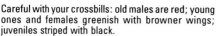

juvenile

old male

female

Careful with your crossbills: old males are red; young ones and females greenish with browner wings; juveniles striped with black.

Tree pipits sing from big trees beside clearings, also good for crested tits, mistle thrushes. Bilberries among small trees attract black grouse and capercaillies.

Tree pipit

Older pines have nesting crossbills or Scottish crossbills, siskins, redstarts. Long-eared owls prefer forest edge with nearby clearings; tawny commoner in forest.

Long-eared owl

Ptarmigan are tame, sometimes elusive, on high plateaux. Cliffs repay scrutiny with ravens, ring ouzels, maybe eagles and peregrines.

213

Semi-Arctic mountain plateau

Northern and western mountains in Scotland and Scandinavia have country similar to the Arctic tundra at quite low altitudes. Southern and central European mountain ranges need to be much higher to achieve the long-lasting snow cover and bleak, windswept conditions that exclude all but the hardiest birds.

On distant peaks, little will be seen in winter except on the finest days, when golden eagles and ravens may soar above the summits. In summer, even swifts, gulls and crows do so.

Purple sandpiper

Snowy owls are rare birds of the tundra, exceptionally recorded on mountains. In Scandinavia there are purple sandpipers and Temminck's stints.

Ring ouzel

Wheatear

In summer ring ouzels visit the high crags and even wheatears nest at high levels, but in winter small birds are virtually absent.

Lapland bunting, female

Snow buntings breed in the very few rocky corries where the snow remains unmelted well into summer. They are widespread in winter. Rarely, a Lapland bunting or shore lark appears.

On the mountains of central Europe there are snowfinches and wallcreepers, both absent from Britain.

Raven

Dotterel

summer female

The high, rocky plateau with short vegetation and patches of snow is ideal ptarmigan ground. Dotterels are only there in the summer, on the broader ridges.

Ptarmigan
spring
male

Golden eagle

Golden eagles hunt over high peaks, for ptarmigan and mountain hares, but nest lower down in sheltered valleys where the nesting ledges are free from snow.

North-western mountain and forest

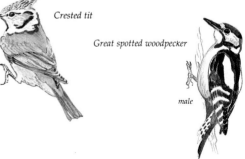

Crested tit

Great spotted woodpecker

male

Birches visited by redpolls when seed is ripe: they feed underneath when seed falls to ground in winter. Crested tits favour old pine woods with rotten stumps.

Scottish hills and mountains have a bird life and character of their own: rocky peaks and extensive deer forest fall away into forested valleys with deep lochs.

Sharp skyline worth watching for golden eagles, ravens. Buzzards frequently lower, over woods and valley slopes – eagles often keep higher up nearer the peaks.

Buzzard   *Golden eagle*

Large lochs may have both red-throated and black-throated divers nesting. Black-throats fish in the breeding loch and nest on islands. Stony lake edge good for common sandpipers, more rarely dippers.

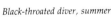

Black-throated diver, summer

Conifers have siskins, redpolls, great spotted woodpeckers. Sunny clearings have spotted flycatchers; along the forest edge robins, chaffinches, tawny or long-eared owls.

Goldeneye

Goosander

Goldeneyes nest around lochs in hollow trees (or nestboxes); goosanders in trees near rivers where they fish. Greylag geese may visit the lochs from time to time.

male

Mountain and valley

High ground with mixed habitats in the valleys can be exciting birdwatching country, because a short walk from the hill to the lake samples several types of terrain.

Stock dove

Raven

Peregrine, adult

The crags above wild corries are used by nesting peregrines and ravens. Stock doves and jackdaws nest in cliffs and quarries.

High moors are hunted by buzzards, rarely golden eagles. A few golden plovers nest on level ground with burned heather, grass or bilberry swards.

Jackdaw

Watch for crossbills in the larches (but only present in a good year). Large forests beside lakes and moors are likely places for sparrowhaws and, in a few places, goshawks too.

Goldeneye

male

Stony shores have common sandpipers in spring and autumn, and all summer if they nest. Deep, acid lakes are not healthy bird sites, but attract mallards, teal and, in winter, goldeneyes.

Stony streams attract few birds except those living nearby that may go to drink and bathe – so approach carefully in case something is there.

Ravens love windswept, open spaces in high hills. Bracken slopes are full of whinchats. Flocks of young starlings move up to the moors at the end of the summer.

Improved, fertilized fields are not especially interesting, except for some nesting lapwings and skylarks, and probably foraging magpies.

Crag and scree above acid lake

Many mountain sites are rather poor for birds, but particular landscape features, such as a cliff or scree slope, add an element of variety and excitement.

Stock dove

Black-headed gull

Peregrine

winter

Ring ouzel

Raven

These mountain cliffs seem unlikely spots for stock doves, but they, and jackdaws, are quite frequent. Choughs are very rare.

Scree slopes (with short grass) are good for wheatears so long as they can feed nearby. Ring ouzels go for a mix of scree and big, tumbling boulders with heather or bracken.

Ravens nest on crags, usually impossible to reach beneath an overhang. Many crags have peregrines on them.

Wheatear

The deep, cold, acid pool attracts few birds beyond drinking or bathing black-headed gulls or common sandpipers.

Golden plovers go right to the top of most hills, as do skylarks and meadow pipits. Curlews probe in the sphagnum moss of upland moors.

Poor quality heather, mixed with rough grass and cotton grass, has few red grouse but there may be golden plovers and even a pair of dunlins in a wet flush.

Golden plover

winter

northern

southern

summer

High central European mountains

Alpine peaks provide a habitat in central Europe with conditions suitable for birds of the Arctic tundra, but there are also species here found no further north. Below the high peaks, flowery meadows and high-altitude forest add a mixed, intricate environment for birds.

Alpine accentor

Highest alpine meadows and screes attract Alpine accentors. In summer wallcreepers nest on undisturbed shady crags. Choughs and alpine choughs feed, golden eagles hunt here.

Remote, sharp peaks have few birds. Alpine choughs move up in summer, hanging around ski lifts. In winter they are in lower meadows. Snowfinches prefer to visit high plateaux.

Nutcracker

Alpine chough

The upper limits of conifer forests are visited by citril finches and black woodpeckers patrol the bigger pines. Nutcrackers often perch on the very tops of big trees before swooping across the valley.

Deep forest may still house rare birds such as capercaillies, three-toed woodpeckers and Tengmalm's owls, all hard to find. Goshawks are easier to see when displaying, honey buzzards shy.

Water pipits favour large, open moorland high on the slopes; meadow pipits inhabit Alpine meadows, tree pipits the woodland fringe, yellow wagtails pastures with grazing cattle.

Meadow pipit

summer

winter

Water pipit

Meadows edged by forest usually have singing ortolans, woodlarks, black redstarts, goldfinches, chaffinches. Forest edge adds firecrest, siskin, willow tit and nutcracker.

Alpine swift

Golden eagle

Lower cliffs are used by wallcreepers in winter. Ravens, golden eagles and peregrines (rare) nest. Alpine swifts, crag martins, black redstarts are typical of deep, craggy valleys.

Mediterranean mountains

Hot summer days and glaring light typify the harsh conditions of many mountainous zones around the Mediterranean. Winter days are cold, windswept and difficult for the birds on these hills.

Griffon vulture

Vultures roam widely over the bare upper slopes. Griffons are the commonest vultures in Europe; Egyptians widespread; black vultures now very rare and found only in Majorca and central Iberia.

The barest slopes may have the rare spectacled warbler; low, thick scrub Dartfords and (rare) Marmora's; taller bushes bring in subalpine and Sardinian warblers too, and olives or orchards add orphean warblers and blackcaps to the list.

immature

Bonelli's warbler

male

Dartford warbler

immature

Jingling corn buntings and sizzling serins add their voices to the crickets' and cicadas' on the hot bushy slopes. Sardinian warblers, cirl buntings and woodlarks are typical inhabitants.

Almost any wet place will attract noisy Cetti's warblers, but drier, grassy tracts are needed by fan-tailed warblers. Stony fields and bushy slopes often have stone-curlews.

GOLDFINCH

adult and immature

juvenile

adult

Watch out for young goldfinches: the wings are similar to adults', only duller black, but head is drab grey, without red, black and white.

The goldfinch is the spirit of the Mediterranean, flashing yellow as flocks dance across the seeding thistles and weedy field edges, often joined by serins.

Black vulture

dark

pale

Eleonora's falcon

Over mountains and gorges on Mediterranean islands, Eleonora's falcons patrol daily from late spring to late autumn, picking off migrant birds around crowded coastal cliffs.

Serin

Firecrests and Bonelli's warblers breed in oakwoods and dry conifer forest, while nightingales prefer damper, shadier spots and dense hedgerows beside cultivation.

High southern mountains

Bare, rocky peaks and snowfields rise above extensive flowery slopes and stone-walled pastures in the high Pyrenees. Below are coniferous and beech woods, cliffs and fast-flowing rivers.

In spring, high altitude streams and boggy patches attract migrant common sandpipers and little ringed plovers. Shoreline waders pause to rest alongside parties of wagtails.

Look skywards in spring and autumn to see migrating honey buzzards, black kites, white and (rare) black storks and kestrels; vast numbers of swallows, swifts, pigeons and doves migrate closer to ground level.

Honey buzzard

Black kite

Extensive screes have many black redstarts, easy to hear but hard to spot, and often even more elusive Alpine accentors. Choughs and Alpine choughs may be found together on crags or feeding beside wet, green flushes.

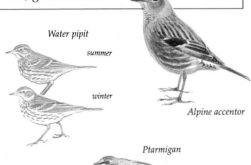

Water pipit

summer

winter

Alpine accentor

Ptarmigan

autumn male

Small birds are often mistaken for larger ones and vice versa in this environment where the awesome scale and vast empty spaces make judgement of size and distance very difficult.

Peregrines occupy some of the sheer crags, sometimes close to ravens, kestrels and eagles. Griffon vultures nest much lower but soar up to the higher peaks for food.

On the tops, a few ptarmigan survive, hunted by golden eagles. Snowfinches haunt the snowy corries and peaks; wallcreepers go right to the highest snow-free crags in summer.

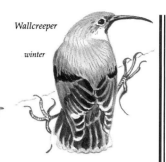

Wallcreeper

winter

Ortolan bunting

Rock thrush

Grassy slopes with scattered boulders and wet hollows are perfect for water pipits, wheatears, rock thrushes, choughs and ortolan buntings.

Southern mountain lake and forest

Southern France rises to a cooler, greener face of the Pyrenees than the hot, arid slopes of the waves of foothills on the Spanish side. The high forests and open slopes have similar birds, with some of the warm-weather specialities missing.

Honey buzzards pass overhead on migration and a few breed in the woods if left alone. There are kestrels and hobbies and occasional short-toed eagles.

Forests of large pines have interesting birds which are difficult to glimpse, including black woodpeckers, capercaillies, goshawks and eagle owls.

Capercaillie

male

Bonelli's warblers, firecrests, crested tits, blackcaps, short-toed treecreepers and chaffinches are easy to find; citril finches are difficult, and at higher altitudes.

Bonelli's warbler adult

The higher open slopes have tree pipits, woodlarks and ortolan buntings. Rock buntings favour screes and boulders, as do rock thrushes, wheatears and ring ouzels.

Ortolan bunting

The lakes and their shores have rather few birds; grey and white wagtails, a few common sandpipers, great crested grebes and coots.

Short-toed eagle
adult

hovering

Grassy meadows by the lake are worth exploring for yellow wagtails, whinchats and crested larks. Hoopoes often add a flash of colour; cuckoos are often heard.

Chaffinch

female

Southern mountain gorge

The foothills of the Pyrenees on the Spanish side are hot in summer, often very cold and windswept in winter. Many sheltered gorges and sheer cliffs give secure nest sites to birds of prey and mountain birds.

Dry, aromatic scrub above the gorge has rock thrushes, firecrests, Sardinian and subalpine warblers. Dartford warblers are in the short vegetation, Bonelli's warblers in the trees.

Alpine swifts feed in and above the gorge; crag and house martins are common about the rock faces. Wallcreepers spend the winter and sometimes nest in these cliffs.

Rock thrush, male

Alpine swift

The cliff ledges and caves are used by griffon and Egyptian vultures. Lammergeiers are frequently seen over gorges and nearby peaks. Bonelli's eagles (very rare) may be found.

Blue rock thrushes sing from the crags and rock sparrows are elusive in surrounding rocks. Black redstarts, serins and cirl buntings are frequently heard and seen.

Griffon vulture

Egyptian vulture

Chough

Birds of prey are many and varied, from peregrines to golden, short-toed and booted eagles, also red and black kites. Choughs are common: they are often in sizeable flocks.

Blue rock thrush
male

The wood in the bottom of the gorge has jays, blackbirds, treecreepers, firecrests, nightingales and Cetti's warblers. Great spotted woodpeckers are common.

Hot mountain foothills

Northern Spain, on the edge of the Pyrenees, is characterized by broad valleys with deeply incised rivers and bare, badland topography around isolated hills. The birds are wonderful and very varied.

The hilltop village abounds with swifts and swallows. In its walls rock sparrows and black redstarts breed; at dusk, scops owls emerge to call from wires and rooftops.

Scops owl

Swift

Black redstart

spring male

Subalpine warbler

immature

Thick bushes hidden in sheltered gullies ring to the song of nightingales; there are melodious and subalpine warblers, blackbirds, linnets and stonechats.

Cereal fields have quails and red-legged partridges. Overhead are Montagu's harriers, short-toed and booted eagles, griffon and Egyptian vultures, as well as kestrels and hobbies.

Booted eagle

pale

Quail

Spotless starlings nest in old roofs and fly to feed on nearby pastures. The grassy, stony slopes are typical habitat for wheatears and rock thrushes, cirl buntings and serins.

Corn buntings are abundant around bushy slopes and cereal fields. Hoopoes are rather scarce; crested larks and tawny pipits frequent. Red and black kites are numerous.

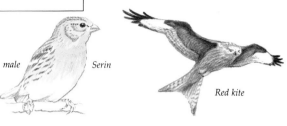

male   Serin

Red kite

Ortolan bunting, spring male

Valley slopes are good for ortolan buntings and woodlarks. In poplars there are golden orioles. Woodchat shrikes are widespread, whereas red-backed shrikes prefer the higher valleys.

Black kite

Where to see birds in Europe: the highlights

A black guillemot.

Seabirds

There are many outstanding seabird cliffs around Scotland and Ireland, including the **Cliffs of Moher, Co Clare** and the **Blasket Islands** and **The Skelligs of Co Kerry; St Kilda** in the Western Isles, **Handa Island** and **Cape Wrath** at the north-western corner of Scotland and a long list of splendid reserves with big colonies in Orkney and Shetland including **Marwick Head, Hoy, Copinsay, Foula,** and **Hermaness.** On the Scottish east coast, the **Bass Rock, Troup Head** and **Fowlsheugh** are memorable sites, while farther south **Bempton Cliffs** nature reserve is magnificent for its kittiwakes and guillemots, as well as some gannets.

South-west Wales has beautiful island reserves full of seabirds in **Skomer, Skokholm** and **Grassholm,** not only with gannets and auks to see by day, but huge numbers of Manx shearwaters which arrive in an incomparable cacophony of calls at night.

There are seabird cliffs in the Channel Islands and north-west France, including **Les Sept-Iles,** while Norway has a string of important islands including **Runde** and **Røst.**

Some exciting seabird-watching stations are to be found on many western headlands, where ocean-going species can be watched as they come close inshore, especially in gales. **Cape Clear Island** and **Brandon Point** in south-west Ireland, **St Ives** and **Porthgwarra** in Cornwall, **Strumble Head** in Wales, **Ardnamurchan Point** and many other Scottish headlands, also **Flamborough Head** and others in the North Sea all provide, in the right conditions, days of thrilling birdwatching. There are opportunities, too, for seabird watching in Brittany.

Birds of estuaries and coastal wetlands

Around southern and eastern Ireland there is a string of important estuary and marsh reserves with great congregations of geese, ducks and waders. **Cork Harbour, Bannow Bay, Tacumshin, Wexford Harbour** and **Wexford Slobs, Lough Foyle** and **Strangford Lough** are all fine bird areas. Across the Irish Sea lie **Morecambe Bay,** the **Alt estuary,** the **Dee** and the **Mersey,** making the greater Liverpool Bay area among the most vital of all coastal habitats for migrant water birds. To the north is the **Solway** and to the south the **Severn,** and then a long line of southern and eastern British estuaries – the **Exe, Chichester** and **Langstone Harbours,** the whole **North Kent, Thames and Essex complex,** the **Wash** and the **Humber** are all of immense value.

The shallow seas and inlets of Denmark are enormously important for breeding and wintering estuary birds. The brackish **Ulvedybet** lake has hundreds of breeding terns and avocets and thousands of swans, ducks and waders in winter. **Ålborg Bugt** boasts 55,000 eiders and tens of thousands of scoters and other sea ducks. **South Laesø** and the adjacent sea is a breeding area for hundreds of avocets and terns, and outside the breeding season is home to 80,000 eiders, tens of thousands of common and velvet scoters and hundreds of avocets. In fact these are just a few of the many such excellent sites in a country famous for its wetlands.

The eastern shores of the North Sea have many superb bird areas. The **Waddensee** rates among the world's best estuarine sites, with vast numbers of waders, geese and ducks, also significant numbers of nesting Sandwich, common and little terns. The adjacent **Dollart** in Germany can have up to 19,000 avocets (making England's Minsmere look like small beer by comparison), 50,000 dunlins and geese galore. Between the Ems and the Elbe, in the **Nationalpark Niedersächsisches Wattenmeer,** geese include 9,000 brents as well as beans, barnacles, pink-feet and greylags. There are 85,000 shelducks during their communal moult, 20,000 eiders, 42,000 oystercatchers, 10,000 avocets,

120,000 dunlins – just a selection of the staggering bird populations of this vast, but severely threatened, wilderness of mud, sea and sand.

The flat, sandy coasts of Schleswig-Holstein in northern Germany are especially valued for their tens of thousands of long-tailed ducks, eiders, scoters and goldeneyes and in summer many terns nest along the beautiful beaches.

Around the **IJselmeer** and **Texel** in the Netherlands there are excellent places for wildfowl, with some wonderful gatherings of tufted ducks, pochards, goosanders, smews and eiders and many of the waders characteristic of the Waddensee. The Polderlands and older pastures have very large numbers of barnacle, white-fronted and bean geese, as well as whooper and Bewick's swans. Texel is known as an 'island of birds', with lovely nature reserves and an abundance of birdwatching opportunities.

In France, notable estuaries include the **Seine,** the **Somme, Baie des Veys** in Normandy, **Baie du Mont-St-Michel** – superb for grey plovers, dunlins, godwits, oystercatchers and wigeons – and a variety of bays and estuaries in Brittany.

Special wetlands

Wetland reserves are among the most interesting of European bird sites. In Britain there are the **Ouse Washes,** with enormous concentrations of wigeon and large flocks of wintering Bewick's swans. The Lancashire mosses have big concentrations of pink-footed geese while more northern sites, such as **Loch Leven** and the **Loch of Strathbeg** in Scotland, are spectacular when great flocks of geese fly in to roost every autumn and winter. **Islay,** in the Inner Hebrides, is home to well over 20,000 barnacle geese in winter, as well as many other geese, wildfowl, waders and birds of prey.

In eastern England, and at **Leighton Moss** in Lancashire in particular, a few reed bed reserves remain, with bitterns, marsh harriers and bearded tits. **Minsmere, Walberswick, Cley Marshes** and **Titchwell** are all interesting East Anglian examples. Inland reservoirs, for example **Rutland Water, Chew Valley Lake** and **Abberton,** have all become splendid wildfowl sites and give many satisfying days' all-round birdwatching.

Northern European wetlands include an important wader breeding area at **Havmyran,** the **Jæren** wetlands of Rogaland with many wildfowl and wintering grebes and divers, and also **Nordre Øyeren** in Norway. Sweden has fine lakes in the south at **Lake Krankesjön** and near **Kristianstad,** where bitterns, harriers, crakes, ruffs, black-tailed godwits and black terns nest. **Lake Åsnen,** Kronoberg, is wonderful for large numbers of breeding divers and ospreys and **Lake Kävsjön,** Jönköping, has divers, grebes, swans and other wildfowl, cranes and many waders breeding. But there are many other lake and wet meadow sites in Scandinavia which are worth exploration.

In the Netherlands, the vast reed bed reserves on the Polderlands are marvellous all year round, with avocets, bluethroats, great colonies of cormorants and many more species in summer, plus harriers, rough-legged buzzards and geese in winter, and a host of terns, gulls and waders during migration. The **Oostvardersplassen** and **Harderbroek** near Lelystad are particularly good, and nearby waterways in winter are full of smews, goosanders and other diving ducks.

The **Lauwersmeer** in the north has its ducks and waders, too, but is especially famous for great flocks of barnacle geese every winter. The **Nardermeer,** a freshwater lake with swampy forests, has huge numbers of nesting cormorants as well as a few bitterns and many grey and purple herons, spoonbills and black terns. Special wet meadow reserves on Texel and near Lelystad show how rich much of the Netherlands used to be, with breeding black-tailed godwits and ruffs.

Adjacent to the Schleswig-Holstein coastal sites, with their massive waterfowl populations, there are also lakes with breeding bitterns, white storks, marsh and Montagu's harriers, spotted crakes, godwits and terns and numerous migrants. There are many reed beds, lakes and shallows along the Rhine where wetland birds are still numerous and varied, as at **Lampertheimer Altrhein** and **Kühkopf-Knoblauchsaue.** The Danube valley retains a few such sites, as at **Donau-Tal,** Bayern.

In France, the wetland that dominates all others is, of course, the **Camargue,** with its magnificent flamingos and a wonderful selection of wetland and Mediterranean species, including such southern specialities as little egrets, squacco herons, whiskered terns and black-winged stilts. Spain is similarly famous for one major wetland, the **Coto Doñana,** where

Where to see birds/2

you can watch flamingos, purple gallinules, spoonbills and egrets alongside such a wide variety of species as pin-tailed sandgrouse, imperial eagles, red and black kites, bee-eaters and lesser short-toed, short-toed, crested and thekla larks. Spain has many other wetlands of huge importance, many tragically threatened, with a markedly different variety of birds from any in north-western Europe: in fact, Iberia deserves a volume to itself.

The forests

In Britain, one forest area is of remarkable significance: the ancient Caledonian pines of **Speyside** and **Deeside**. They have the only species that is found in Britain and nowhere else in the world, the Scottish crossbill, as well as ospreys, golden eagles, capercaillies, black grouse and crested tits. Elsewhere in Britain the woods are full of warblers, woodpeckers, treecreepers, and, in the south, nuthatches, with significant areas for localized species such as pied flycatchers, wood warblers and others. The **New Forest** combines woods with heath and bog, and is excellent for hobbies, Dartford warblers and nightjars as well as woodland birds proper.

Northern forests in Scandinavia are often quite different. The mountains of **Vindelfjällen** in Sweden have great pine and birch forests with eagles, gyr falcons, eagle owls and Arctic warblers. In Finland there are great grey and Ural owls, white-backed and three-toed woodpeckers, but the mature, virgin forests which these species need are now few and far between.

In much of Europe the woods are dominated by oak and beech and have black, great spotted, middle spotted, green and grey-headed woodpeckers, nuthatches, treecreepers and short-toed treecreepers, goldcrests and firecrests. Characteristic predators are goshawks, sparrowhawks, buzzards and honey buzzards. Red and black kites forage around woodland edges and clearings. In a few places, black storks and hazel hens nest.

Mediterranean woods and many in southern and western France have species that prefer warm, dry places: Bonelli's, orphean, Sardinian and subalpine warblers, hoopoes, black and red kites, booted and short-toed eagles, serins and woodlarks. Alpine forests have their particular birds, too, with citril finches and nutcrackers among others.

WORTH A SPECIAL JOURNEY

The bulk of this book is about extensive, widespread habitats, but much good birdwatching is available at specially managed nature reserves. To single out individual places from the enormous number of bird sites in western Europe is, in some ways, beside the point, but some are so good that they are indeed worth a special journey – or just dreaming about. So the list which follows is an attempt to define the cream of European birdwatching. Starred sites are the *crème de la crème*.

Seabirds
*Grassholm, Skomer (Wales); *St Kilda, *Hermaness, Fetlar, Fair Isle, *Fowlsheugh, *Bass Rock (Scotland); *Bempton Cliffs (England); Cliffs of Moher, Blasket Islands, Puffin Island, *The Skelligs (Ireland); Les Sept-Iles (France); *Varangefjord, Røst, Runde (Norway).

Marine wildfowl, geese
Dornoch Firth, Moray Firth, Solway, *Islay, *Loch of Strathbeg, *Loch Leven (Scotland); Martin Mere, Lindisfarne, Slimbridge (England); *Wexford Slobs, Strangford Lough (Ireland); *Ålborg Bugt, *South Laesø, *Randers Fjord, *Horsens Fjord, *Stavns Fjord, Ringkøbing Fjord, Sejerø Bugt, Roskilde Fjord, Lillebaelt (Denmark); Baie du Mont-St-Michel, *Golfe du Morbihan (France); *Schleswig-Holsteinisches Wattenmeer, *Nationalpark Niedersächsisches Wattenmeer, Küste der Probstei, Traveförde und Dassower See, Westrügen, *Hiddensee, *Greifswalder Bodden, Niederrhein (Germany); *Waddensee, *IJselmeer, *Texel, Sneekermeer, Grevelingen, Oosterswchelde (Netherlands).

Estuaries
*Morecame Bay, *The Wash, *Ribble, *Alt, Dee, Humber, Thames (England); *Solway, Forth (Scotland); *Seine, Baie du Mont-St-Michel, Loire, Baie de l'Aiguillon, Golfe du Morbihan, Etier de Penerf, Ile d'Oleron (France); Beneden Schelde (Belgium); *Wattenmeer, Dollart, *Greifswalder Bodden (Germany); *Waddensee, *Oosterschelde, Westerschelde (Netherlands).

Special wetlands
Ouse Washes, Somerset Levels, Minsmere, Leighton Moss (England); *Camargue, *Lac du Der-Chantecoq, *Lac de la Foret d'Orient, La Brenne, Sologne des etangs foret de Bruadan,

Etang de Galetas, Baie des Veys, Val d'Allier, Vallee de la Scarpe, La Chaussee, Lac de Madine, La Dombes, Etangs de Bages, Etangs du Languedoc (France); Het Zwin, West-Vlaanderen (Belgium); *Nardermeer, *Oostvardersplassen, Lauwersmeer, De Wieden, Van Oordt's Merksen, Ijsseldelta, *Zuidelijk Poldergebied (Netherlands); Ostufer Muritz, Galenbecker See, Untere Havelniederung, Unterer Inn, Untersee, Rheinauen (Germany); Vejlerne, Maribo Lakes, Tystrup, Tissø, Arresø (Denmark).

Mountains

*Cairngorms (Scotland); Rhone-Alpes, Auvergne, Provence Alpes, Gavarnie (Pyrenees) (France); Bayern Alps, Nationalpark Berchtesgaden (Germany); Haute Fagnes, Eifel (Belgium); *Hardangervidda, Dovrefjell (Norway); *Vindelfjällen, Påkketan (Sweden); Alps, Jura (Switzerland).

Forests and heaths

Arne Heath, Studland Heath, New Forest, Thetford Forest, Forest of Dean (England); *Speyside, *Deeside (Scotland); Gwenffrwd/Dinas, Mawddach Valley (Wales); Foret d'Orient, Foret d'Iraty, Foret d'Issaux, Pyrenees-Orientales, Midi-Pyrenees, Auvergne, Corbières, Montagne Sainte Victoire (France); Nationalpark Berchtesgaden, Karwendel, Ammergauer Bergeuhlstader Heide, Elbsandsteingebirge (Germany); Meynweg, Fochteloerveen, Vennen van Oisterijk, Holterberg (Netherlands); *Ovre Pasvik (Norway); Falsterbo, Ottenby, Påkketan, Sjaunja (Sweden).

Migration watchpoints and hotspots

*Falsterbo, Öland (Sweden); *Fair Isle (Scotland); *Isles of Scilly, Flamborough Head, Cley/Blakeney/ Wells, Dungeness, Portland Bill (England); Bardsey, Skokholm (Wales); Cape Clear Island, Tacumshin, Ballycotton (Ireland); Texel, Vlieland, Terschelling (Netherlands); Flagbakken, Skagen, Råbjerg Mile (Denmark); Ile d'Ouessant (France); Heligoland (Germany).

Full details of locations and which species to expect are available in an extremely useful book entitled *Important Bird Areas of Europe* by Grimmett and Jones, published by the International Council for Bird Preservation. For details of access, permits and ownership of reserves in the U.K., see *The Birdwatcher's Yearbook*, another useful publication, edited by John E. Pemberton, from Buckingham Press, 25 Manor Park, Maids Moreton, Buckingham MK18 1QX.

INDEX

of species mentioned on the landscape photograph spreads, pages 24-233.

The RSPB

The Royal Society for the Protection of Birds is the major charity in the U.K. that takes action to conserve wild birds and the places where they live, an aim which this book also serves by emphasizing the crucial link between birds and their natural habitats. The work of the RSPB centres around research to find out the precise requirements of wild birds, including crucial features of their natural habitat, followed by action to ensure that those requirements remain fulfilled in the modern world.

The RSPB has a network of over 120 nature reserves which provide properly managed sites for most species of breeding and wintering birds that can be found in Britain and Northern Ireland. Rare breeding birds, such as avocets, marsh harriers, bitterns, corncrakes and black-tailed godwits, find ideal conditions in RSPB nature reserves. Important wintering and migrant birds, including wigeons, barnacle geese, knots, dunlins and grey plovers, have safe refuges on RSPB wetland and estuary reserves. Seabirds, with which Britain is particularly blessed, nest undisturbed on a network of coastal cliffs and island reserves.

Reserves alone are insufficient to maintain the wealth of wildlife across the U.K. countryside. The RSPB argues for improved safeguards for habitats and sites of special value and works with planners and decision-makers to prevent conflict between development and conservation. It undertakes a strong and effective educational programme and, recognizing that birds belong to no one and no single country, the RSPB has an expanding international strategy to improve protection for birds in Europe and Africa.

The 850,000 members receive exclusive, award-winning magazines: *BIRDS* or, for the junior section, *BIRD LIFE*. Members have free access to RSPB nature reserves, can join local members' groups and attend shows of highly-acclaimed, RSPB-produced wildlife films.

National headquarters
The Royal Society for the Protection of Birds, The Lodge, Sandy, Bedfordshire SG19 2DL   0767 680551

RSPB Scottish Headquarters
17 Regent Terrace, Edinburgh EH7 5BN   031 557 3136

RSPB Northern Ireland Regional Office
Belvoir Park Forest, Belfast BT8 4QT   0232 491547

RSPB Wales Office
Bryn Aderyn, The Bank, Newtown, Powys SY16 2AB   0686 626678